FRIENDSHIP

POEMS

SELECTED AND
EDITED BY
PETER WASHINGTON

EVERYMAN'S LIBRARY
POCKET POETS

This selection by Peter Washington first published in
Everyman's Library, 1995
© David Campbell Publishers Ltd., 1995

A list of acknowledgments to copyright owners can be found at the back of
this volume.

ISBN 1-85715-719-2

A CIP catalogue record for this book is available from the British Library

Published by David Campbell Publishers Ltd.,
79 Berwick Street, London W1V 3PF

Distributed by Random House (UK) Ltd.,
20 Vauxhall Bridge Road, London SW1V 2SA

Typography by Peter B. Willberg

Typeset by MS Filmsetting Ltd., Frome, Somerset

Printed and bound in Germany by
Mohndruck Graphische Betriebe GmbH, Gütersloh

CONTENTS

POETS TOGETHER

STRANGERS

9

LOOKING BACK

FOREWORD

This collection of poems about friendship is the third in a series of Everyman anthologies dealing with aspects of love. My only difficulty when compiling *Love Poems* was how to select from the huge quantity of first-rate material available. As might be expected, *Erotic Poems* presented me with rather more problems of taste and judgment. Curiously, though, *Friendship Poems* has been the most perplexing of the three to assemble. Perhaps because friendship is usually a less dramatic part of life than passion, it is less likely to inspire incandescent verse. Yet, for many people, friendship is no less important than passion. It often turns out to be more enduring and profound, and even the most ardent lovers may find companionship outliving desire.

For convenience of arrangement the poems have once again been divided into categories.

PETER WASHINGTON

WHAT ARE FRIENDS?

NATURE ASSIGNS THE SUN

Nature assigns the Sun –
That – is Astronomy –
Nature cannot enact a Friend –
That – is Astrology.

FRIENDSHIP

Such love I cannot analyse;
It does not rest in lips or eyes,
Neither in kisses nor caress.
Partly, I know, it's gentleness

And understanding in one word
Or in brief letters. It's preserved
By trust and by respect and awe.
These are the words I'm feeling for.

Two people, yes, two lasting friends.
The giving comes, the taking ends.
There is no measure for such things.
For this all Nature slows and sings.

QUARRELLING

The ancients argued that friendship could never last.
A few old friends, we walk on the mountain's
    milder slopes,
Discussing their reasons. The wind lifts our coats.
An hour passes, and we find we are shaking our staffs,
We are out of breath. We must have been quarrelling!
Some prophecies, if you listen to them, come true.
Quickly we drop the topic, open the picnic baskets,
And pour the wine. How sad it would be to drink alone!
Someone recites a poem on the sorrow of separation.
It seems the famous sages were not unfailingly right.

FRIENDSHIP

If you're ever in a jam,
    Here I am.
If you're ever in a mess,
    S.O.S.
If you ever feel so happy you land in jail,
    I'm your bail.

It's friendship, friendship,
Just a perfect blendship.
When other friendships have been forgot,
Ours will still be hot.

If you're ever up a tree,
    Phone to me.
If you're ever down a well,
    Ring my bell.
If you ever lost your teeth and you're out to dine,
    Borrow mine.

It's friendship, friendship,
Just a perfect blendship.
When other friendships have been forgate,
Ours will still be great.

If they ever black your eyes,
    Put me wise.
If they ever cook your goose,
    Turn me loose.
If they ever put a bullet through your brain,
    I'll complain.

It's friendship, friendship,
Just a perfect blendship.
When other friendships have been forgit,
Ours will still be it.

UNKINDNESS

Lord, make me coy and tender to offend:
In friendship, first I think, if that agree,
        Which I intend,
          Unto my friend's intent and end.
I would not use a friend, as I use Thee.

If any touch my friend, or his good name,
It is my honour and my love to free
        His blasted fame
          From the least spot or thought of blame.
I could not use a friend, as I use Thee.

My friend may spit upon my curious floor:
Would he have gold? I lend it instantly;
        But let the poor,
          And thou within them, starve at door.
I cannot use a friend, as I use Thee.

When that my friend pretendeth to a place,
I quit my interest, and leave it free:
               But when thy grace
                   Sues for my heart, I thee displace.
Nor would I use a friend, as I use Thee.

Yet can a friend what thou hast done fulfil?
O write in brass, *My God upon a tree*
                  His blood did spill
              Only to purchase my good-will.
Yet use I not my foes, as I use Thee.

I WOULD BUT I CAN'T

I would but I can't
make you my friend;

you never ask or give
when I ask or take
what I'd give.

A FRIEND IN NEED WILL BE AROUND
IN FIVE MINUTES

What are friends?
Why, they are people for love of whom one goes out
      and eagerly borrows what one to them eagerly
      lends,
Who in return assure one that if one were about to be
      eaten by an octopus they would dive fathoms deep
      to the rescue at the risk of contracting the bends,
But who, if one faces any more prosaic emergency such
      as asking if they would mind one's bringing along
      an extra girl, one is making a mistake if one on
      them depends.
They are people on whose entertainment one's entire
      income one hospitably and hebdomadally spends,
And who at one's house eat birthright and at their
      house one eats pottage and other odds and ends,
And for whose behaviour one is to one's foes
      constantly making amends,
Yes, that's what are friends.
What then are foes?
Why they are the least of anybody sensible's woes,
Because if there is one thing that you might of anybody
      sensible suppose,
It is that he wouldn't have anything to do with people
      who prove to be foes,

Because obviously if one tarries blithely among one's
    proven foemen,
Why whom has one to blame but oneself if one receives
    a poisoned barb in the small of the back or a
    poisoned comment on the large of the abdomen?
Yes, friends are unavoidable and epidemic and
    therefore friend trouble is forgivable but I have no
    sympathy for him who circles Robin Hood's barn
    and exposes
Himself to foeses.
I maintain that foes are very nice people as long as a
    reasonable distance separates oneself and them,
    whereas a friend in need or in his cups can reach
    you across mountains of glass and lakes of fire,
    with which remark I shall now close,
Simply pausing to add that compared to a friend at the
    front door I find foes at a reasonable distance
    rather restful, and from now on I shall ever think
    of them as *Comme Il Fauts.*

FRIENDSHIP

Like a quetzal plume, a fragrant flower,
friendship sparkles:
like heron plumes, it weaves itself into finery.
Our song is a bird calling out like a jingle:
how beautiful you make it sound!
Here, among flowers that enclose us,
among flowery boughs you are singing.

FOR FRIENDS ONLY
for John and Teckla Clark

Ours yet not ours, being set apart
As a shrine to friendship,
Empty and silent most of the year,
This room awaits from you
What you alone, as visitor, can bring,
A weekend of personal life.

In a house backed by orderly woods,
Facing a tractored sugar-beet country,
Your working hosts engaged to their stint,
You are unlike to encounter
Dragons or romance: were drama a craving,
You would not have come.

Books we do have for almost any
Literate mood, and notepaper, envelopes,
For a writing one (to 'borrow' stamps
Is a mark of ill-breeding):
Between lunch and tea, perhaps a drive;
After dinner, music or gossip.

Should you have troubles (pets will die,
Lovers are always behaving badly)
And confession helps, we will hear it,
Examine and give our counsel:
If to mention them hurts too much,
We shall not be nosey.

Easy at first, the language of friendship
Is, as we soon discover,
Very difficult to speak well, a tongue
With no cognates, no resemblance
To the galimatias of nursery and bedroom,
Court rhyme or shepherd's prose,

And, unless often spoken, soon goes rusty.
Distance and duties divide us,
But absence will not seem an evil
If it make our re-meeting
A real occasion. Come when you can:
Your room will be ready.

In Tum-Tum's reign a tin of biscuits
On the bedside table provided
For nocturnal munching. Now weapons have changed,
And the fashion in appetites:
There, for sunbathers who count their calories,
A bottle of mineral water.

Felicissima notte! May you fall at once
Into a cordial dream, assured
That whoever slept in this bed before
Was also someone we like,
That within the circle of our affection
Also you have no double.

From THE BOOK OF SONGS
OATHS OF FRIENDSHIP

(1)

If you were riding in a coach
And I were wearing a 'li',
And one day we met in the road,
You would get down and bow.
If you were carrying a 'teng'
And I were riding on a horse,
And one day we met in the road
I would get down for you.

(2)

Shang ya!
I want to be your friend
For ever and ever without break or decay.
When the hills are all flat
And the rivers are all dry,
When it lightens and thunders in winter,
When it rains and snows in summer,
When Heaven and Earth mingle –
Not till then will I part from you.

FRIENDSHIP

I think awhile of Love, and while I think,
    Love is to me a world,
    Sole meat and sweetest drink,
    And close connecting link
      'Tween heaven and earth.

I only know it is, not how or why,
    My greatest happiness;
    However hard I try,
    Not if I were to die,
      Can I explain.

I fain would ask my friend how it can be,
    But when the time arrives,
    Then Love is more lovely
    Than anything to me,
      And so I'm dumb.

For if the truth were known, Love cannot speak,
    But only thinks and does;
    Though surely out 'twill leak
    Without the help of Greek,
      Or any tongue.

A man may love the truth and practise it,
 Beauty he may admire,
 And goodness not omit,
 As much as may befit
  To reverence.

But only when these three together meet,
 As they always incline,
 And make one soul the seat,
 And favorite retreat
  Of loveliness;

When under kindred shape, like loves and hates
 And a kindred nature,
 Proclaim us to be mates,
 Exposed to equal fates
  Eternally;

And each may other help, and service do,
 Drawing Love's bands more tight,
 Service he ne'er shall rue
 While one and one make two,
  And two are one;

In such case only doth man fully prove
    Fully as man can do,
    What power there is in Love
    His inmost soul to move
      Resistlessly.

———————

Two sturdy oaks I mean, which side by side,
    Withstand the winter's storm,
    And spite of wind and tide,
    Grow up the meadow's pride,
      For both are strong

Above they barely touch, but undermined
    Down to their deepest source,
    Admiring you shall find
    Their roots are intertwined
      Insep'rably.

RELATIONSHIPS

Understanding must be on both sides,
Confidence with confidence, and every talk
Be like a long and needed walk
When flowers are picked, and almost – asides
Exchanged. Love is always like this
Even when there's no touch or kiss.

There are many kinds of relationships
But this is the best, as Plato said –
Even when it begins in a bed,
The gentle touching of hands and lips –
It is from such kindness friendship is made
Often, a thing not to be repaid

Since there is no price, no counting up
This and that, gift. Humility
Is the essential ability
Before the loved object. Oh, we can sip
Something that tastes almost divine
In such pure sharing – yours and mine.

From THE CHURCH-PORCH

Wit's an unruly engine, wildly striking
Sometimes a friend, sometimes the engineer.
Hast thou the knack? pamper it not with liking:
But if thou want it, buy it not too deare . . .

Thy friend put in thy bosome: wear his eyes
Still in thy heart, that he may see what's there.
If cause require, thou art his sacrifice;
Thy drops of bloud must pay down all his fear:
But love is lost, the way of friendship's gone,
Though *David* had his *Jonathan*, *Christ* his *John*.

LOVE AND FRIENDSHIP

Love is like the wild rose-briar,
Friendship is like the holly-tree –
The holly is dark when the rose-briar blooms
But which will bloom most constantly?

The wild rose-briar is sweet in spring,
Its summer blossoms scent the air;
Yet wait till winter comes again
And who will call the wild-briar fair?

Then scorn the silly rose-wreath now
And deck thee with the holly's sheen,
That when December blights thy brow
He still may leave thy garland green.

EMILY BRONTË (1818–1848)

From FRIENDSHIP

All love is sacred, and the marriage-tie
Hath much of honour and divinity,
But lust, design, or some unworthy ends
May mingle there, which are despised by friends;
Passion hath violent extremes, and thus
All oppositions are contiguous;
So, when the end is served, their love will bate
If friendship make it not more fortunate:
Friendship, that love's elixir, that pure fire
Which burns the clearer 'cause it burns the higher ...
Friendship, like heraldry, is hereby known
Richest when plainest, bravest when alone,
Calm as a virgin, and more innocent
Than sleeping doves are, and as much content
As saints in visions.

ARE FRIENDS DELIGHT OR PAIN?

Are Friends Delight or Pain?
Could Bounty but remain
Riches were good –

But if they only stay
Ampler to fly away
Riches are sad.

MY LOVELY FRIENDS

My lovely friends
How could I change
towards you who
are so beautiful.

I ask you, Sir, to
stand face to face
with me as a friend
would; show me the
favour of your eyes.

TO ME, FAIR FRIEND

To me, fair friend, you never can be old,
For as you were when first your eye I eyed,
Such seems your beauty still. Three winters cold
Have from the forests shook three summers' pride,
Three beauteous springs to yellow autumn turned
In process of the seasons I have seen,
Three April perfumes in three hot Junes burned,
Since first I saw you fresh, which yet are green.
Ah, yet doth beauty, like a dial hand,
Steal from his figure, and no pace perceived;
So your sweet hue, which methinks still doth stand,
Hath motion, and mine eye may be deceived;
    For fear of which, hear this, thou age unbred:
    Ere you were born was beauty's summer dead.

WILLIAM SHAKESPEARE (1564–1616)   39

From FRIENDSHIP

Candid and generous and just,
Boys care but little whom they trust,
　　An error soon corrected –
For who but learns in riper years,
That man, when smoothest he appears,
　　Is most to be suspected?

Who seeks a friend, should come dispos'd
T'exhibit in full bloom disclos'd
　　The graces and the beauties
That form the character he seeks,
For 'tis an union that bespeaks
　　Reciprocated duties.

A man renown'd for repartee
Will seldom scruple to make free
　　With friendship's finest feeling,
Will thrust a dagger at your breast,
And say he wounded you in jest,
　　By way of balm for healing.

Religion should extinguish strife,
And make a calm of human life;
     But friends that chance to differ
On points, which God has left at large,
How fiercely will they meet and charge,
     No combatants are stiffer!

The man that hails you Tom or Jack,
And proves by thumps upon your back
     How he esteems your merit,
Is such a friend, that one had need
Be very much his friend indeed
     To pardon or to bear it.

Oh Friendship! if my soul forgo
Thy dear delights while here below,
     To mortify and grieve me,
May I myself at last appear
Unworthy, base, and insincere,
     Or may my friend deceive me!

WILLIAM COWPER (1731–1800)   41

THE PLEASURES
OF FRIENDSHIP

THE PLEASURES OF FRIENDSHIP

The pleasures of friendship are exquisite,
How pleasant to go to a friend on a visit!
I go to my friend, we walk on the grass,
And the hours and moments like minutes pass.

IF YOU AND I, JULIUS, OLD FRIEND

If you and I, Julius, old friend,
Were granted licence to expend
Time without worry, infinite leisure,
Together to explore life's pleasure,
We'd neither of us bother then
With the ante-rooms of powerful men,
Arrogant busts, ancestral faces,
Or the law's bitter, tedious cases.
No; strolls, gossip, the Colonnade,
Bookshops, the baths, the garden's shade,
The Aqueduct, the exercise-ground,
Would constitute our onerous round.
But, as it is, we, both and each,
Miss the rich life within our reach.
We watch the good sun speed and set,
And the lost day goes down as debt.
Would any man, if he knew how
To live, not do it here and now?

MARTIAL (AD *c.* 40–*c.* 104),
TRANS. JAMES MICHIE

WE TWO BOYS TOGETHER CLINGING

We two boys together clinging,
One the other never leaving,
Up and down the roads going, North and South
    excursions making,
Power enjoying, elbows stretching, fingers clutching,
Arm'd and fearless, eating, drinking, sleeping, loving,
No law less than ourselves owning, sailing, soldiering,
    thieving, threatening,
Misers, menials, priests alarming, air breathing, water
    drinking, on the turf or the sea-beach dancing,
Cities wrenching, ease scorning, statutes mocking,
    feebleness chasing,
Fulfilling our foray.

WALT WHITMAN (1819–1892)

BEING HER FRIEND

Being her friend, I do not care, not I,
   How gods or men may wrong me, beat me down;
Her word's sufficient star to travel by,
   I count her quiet praise sufficient crown.

Being her friend, I do not covet gold,
   Save for a royal gift to give her pleasure;
To sit with her, and have her hand to hold,
   Is wealth, I think, surpassing minted treasure.

Being her friend, I only covet art,
   A white pure flame to search me as I trace
In crooked letters from a throbbing heart,
   The hymn to beauty written on her face.

From AN EPISTLE TO MASTER
JOHN SELDEN

I know to whom I write. Here, I am sure,
Though I am short, I cannot be obscure;
Less shall I for the art or dressing care,
Truth and the Graces best when naked are.
Your book, my Selden, I have read, and much
Was trusted, that you thought my judgement such
To ask it; though in most of works it be
A penance, where a man may not be free,
Rather than office, when it doth or may
Chance that the friend's affection proves allay
Unto this censure. Yours all need doth fly
Of this so vicious humanity,
Than which there is not unto study a more
Pernicious enemy.

BEN JONSON (1572/3–1637)   49

COMPANION – NORTH-EAST DUG-OUT

He talked of Africa,
    That fat and easy man.
I'd but to say a word,
    And straight the tales began.

And when I'd wish to read,
    That man would not disclose
A thought of harm, but sleep;
    Hard-breathing through his nose.

Then when I'd wish to hear
    More tales of Africa,
'Twas but to wake him up,
    And but a word to say

To press a button, and
    Keep quiet; nothing more;
For tales of stretching veldt,
    Kaffir and sullen Boer.

O what a lovely friend!
    O quiet easy life!
I wonder if his sister
    Would care to be my wife . . .

50   IVOR GURNEY (1890–1937)

THE SUNLIGHT ON THE GARDEN

The sunlight on the garden
Hardens and grows cold,
We cannot cage the minute
Within its nets of gold
When all is told
We cannot beg for pardon.

Our freedom as free lances
Advances towards its end;
The earth compels, upon it
Sonnets and birds descend;
And soon, my friend,
We shall have no time for dances.

The sky was good for flying
Defying the church bells
And every evil iron
Siren and what it tells:
The earth compels,
We are dying, Egypt, dying

And not expecting pardon,
Hardened in heart anew,
But glad to have sat under
Thunder and rain with you,
And grateful too
For sunlight on the garden.

THIS LIME-TREE BOWER MY PRISON
addressed to Charles Lamb, of the India House, London

Well, they are gone, and here must I remain,
This lime-tree bower my prison! I have lost
Beauties and feelings, such as would have been
Most sweet to my remembrance even when age
Had dimm'd mine eyes to blindness! They, meanwhile,
Friends, whom I never more may meet again,
On springy heath, along the hill-top edge,
Wander in gladness, and wind down, perchance,
To that still roaring dell, of which I told;
The roaring dell, o'erwooded, narrow, deep,
And only speckled by the mid-day sun;
Where its slim trunk the ash from rock to rock
Flings arching like a bridge; – that branchless ash,
Unsunn'd and damp, whose few poor yellow leaves
Ne'er tremble in the gale, yet tremble still,
Fann'd by the water-fall! and there my friends
Behold the dark green file of long lank weeds,
That all at once (a most fantastic sight!)
Still nod and drip beneath the dripping edge
Of the blue clay-stone.

Now, my friends emerge
Beneath the wide wide Heaven – and view again
The many-steepled tract magnificent
Of hilly fields and meadows, and the sea,
With some fair bark, perhaps, whose sails light up
The slip of smooth clear blue betwixt two Isles
Of purple shadow! Yes! they wander on
In gladness all; but thou, methinks, most glad,
My gentle-hearted Charles! for thou hast pined
And hunger'd after Nature, many a year,
In the great City pent, winning thy way
With sad yet patient soul, through evil and pain
And strange calamity! Ah! slowly sink
Behind the western ridge, thou glorious Sun!
Shine in the slant beams of the sinking orb,
Ye purple heath-flowers! richlier burn, ye clouds!
Live in the yellow light, ye distant groves!
And kindle, thou blue Ocean! So my friend
Struck with deep joy may stand, as I have stood,
Silent with swimming sense; yea, gazing round
On the wide landscape, gaze till all doth seem
Less gross than bodily; and of such hues
As veil the Almighty Spirit, when yet he makes
Spirits perceive his presence.

          A delight
Comes sudden on my heart, and I am glad
As I myself were there! Nor in this bower,
This little lime-tree bower, have I not mark'd
Much that has sooth'd me. Pale beneath the blaze
Hung the transparent foliage; and I watch'd
Some broad and sunny leaf, and lov'd to see
The shadow of the leaf and stem above
Dappling its sunshine! And that walnut-tree
Was richly ting'd, and a deep radiance lay
Full on the ancient ivy, which usurps
Those fronting elms, and now, with blackest mass
Makes their dark branches gleam a lighter hue
Through the late twilight: and though now the bat
Wheels silent by, and not a swallow twitters,
Yet still the solitary humble-bee
Sings in the bean-flower! Henceforth I shall know
That Nature ne'er deserts the wise and pure;
No plot so narrow, be but Nature there,
No waste so vacant, but may well employ
Each faculty of sense, and keep the heart
Awake to Love and Beauty! and sometimes
'Tis well to be bereft of promis'd good,
That we may lift the soul, and contemplate
With lively joy the joys we cannot share.
My gentle-hearted Charles! when the last rook
Beat its straight path along the dusky air

Homewards, I blest it! deeming its black wing
(Now a dim speck, now vanishing in light)
Had cross'd the mighty Orb's dilated glory,
While thou stood'st gazing; or, when all was still,
Flew creeking o'er thy head, and had a charm
For thee, my gentle-hearted Charles, to whom
No sound is dissonant which tells of Life.

SITTING AT NIGHT

A quiet valley with no man's footprints,
An empty garden lit by the moon.
Suddenly my dog barks and I know
A friend with a bottle is knocking at the gate.

From THE CHOICE

That life may be more comfortable yet,
And all my joys refined, sincere, and great,
I'd choose two friends, whose company would be
A great advance to my felicity:
Well-born, of humours suited to my own,
Discreet, and men as well as books have known;
Brave, gen'rous, witty, and exactly free
From loose behaviour, or formality;
Airy and prudent, merry, but not light,
Quick in discerning, and in judging right.
Secret they should be, faithful to their trust;
In reas'ning cool, strong, temperate, and just;
Obliging, open, without huffing brave,
Brisk in gay talking, and in sober, grave;
Close in dispute, but not tenacious; tried
By solid reason, and let that decide;
Not prone to lust, revenge, or envious hate,
Nor busy meddlers with intrigues of state;
Strangers to slander, and sworn foes to spite,
Not quarrelsome, but stout enough to fight;
Loyal, and pious, friends to Caesar; true,
As dying martyrs, to their Maker too.
In their society I could not miss
A permanent, sincere, substantial bliss.

58   JOHN POMFRET (1667–1702)

AT LEMMONS
for Jane, Kingsley, Colin, Sargy with much love

Above my table three magnolia flowers
Utter their silent requiems.
Through the window I see your elms
In labour with the racking storm
Giving it shape in April's shifty airs.

Up there sky boils from a brew of cloud
To blue gleam, sunblast, then darkens again.
No respite is allowed
The watching eye, the natural agony.

Below is the calm a loved house breeds
Where four have come together to dwell
– Two write, one paints, the fourth invents –
Each pursuing a natural bent
But less through nature's formative travail
Than each in his own humour finding the self he needs.

Round me all is amenity, a bloom of
Magnolia uttering its requiems,
A climate of acceptance. Very well
I accept my weakness with my friends'
Good natures sweetening every day my sick room.

C. DAY LEWIS (1904–1972)   59

MY OLD FRIEND PREPARED
A CHICKEN WITH MILLET

My old friend prepared a chicken with millet,
Inviting me to visit his country home,
Where the green of the trees
Girdles the village
And beyond the walls the blue hills begin.

We opened your windows to inspect the
      kitchen-garden,
Took some wine, and spoke of mulberries and flax.
Wait until the Autumn Festival:
I shall come again,
to enjoy your chrysanthemums.

From AN EPISTLE ANSWERING
TO ONE THAT ASKED TO BE SEALED
OF THE TRIBE OF BEN

Live to that point I will, for which I am man,
    And dwell as in my centre as I can,
Still looking to, and ever loving, heaven;
    With reverence using all the gifts thence given.
'Mongst which, if I have any friendships sent,
    Such as are square, well-tagged, and permanent,
Not built with canvas, paper, and false lights,
    As are the glorious scenes at the great sights,
And that there be no fevery heats, nor colds,
    Oily expansions, or shrunk dirty folds,
But all so clear and led by reason's flame,
    As but to stumble in her sight were shame;
These I will honour, love, embrace, and serve,
    And free it from all question to preserve.
So short you read my character, and theirs
    I would call mine, to which not many stairs
Are asked to climb. First give me faith, who know
    Myself a little. I will take you so,
As you have writ yourself. Now stand, and then,
    Sir, you are sealèd of the tribe of Ben.

GOOD NEIGHBOURS

MENDING WALL

Something there is that doesn't love a wall,
That sends the frozen-ground-swell under it,
And spills the upper boulders in the sun;
And makes gaps even two can pass abreast.
The work of hunters is another thing:
I have come after them and made repair
Where they have left not one stone on a stone,
But they would have the rabbit out of hiding,
To please the yelping dogs. The gaps I mean,
No one has seen them made or heard them made,
But at spring mending-time we find them there.
I let my neighbour know beyond the hill;
And on a day we meet to walk the line
And set the wall between us once again.
We keep the wall between us as we go.
To each the boulders that have fallen to each.
And some are loaves and some so nearly balls
We have to use a spell to make them balance:
'Stay where you are until our backs are turned!'
We wear our fingers rough with handling them.
Oh, just another kind of out-door game,
One on a side. It comes to little more:
There where it is we do not need the wall:
He is all pine and I am apple orchard.
My apple trees will never get across

And eat the cones under his pines, I tell him.
He only says, 'Good fences make good neighbours.'
Spring is the mischief in me, and I wonder
If I could put a notion in his head:
'*Why* do they make good neighbours? Isn't it
Where there are cows? But here there are no cows.
Before I built a wall I'd ask to know
What I was walling in or walling out,
And to whom I was like to give offence.
Something there is that doesn't love a wall,
That wants it down.' I could say 'Elves' to him,
But it's not elves exactly, and I'd rather
He said it for himself. I see him there
Bringing a stone grasped firmly by the top
In each hand, like an old-stone savage armed.
He moves in darkness as it seems to me,
Not of woods only and the shade of trees.
He will not go behind his father's saying,
And he likes having thought of it so well
He says again, 'Good fences make good neighbours.'

NEIGHBOURS

The man that is open of heart to his neighbour,
    And stops to consider his likes and dislikes,
His blood shall be wholesome whatever his labour,
    His luck shall be with him whatever he strikes.
The Splendour of Morning shall duly possess him,
    That he may not be sad at the falling of eve.
And, when he has done with mere living –
        God bless him! –
    A many shall sigh, and one Woman shall grieve!

But he that is costive of soul toward his fellow,
    Through the ways, and the works, and the woes of
        this life,
Him food shall not fatten, him drink shall not mellow;
    And his innards shall brew him perpetual strife.
His eye shall be blind to God's Glory above him;
    His ear shall be deaf to Earth's Laughter around;
His Friends and his Club and his Dog
        shall not love him;
    And his Widow shall skip when he goes
        underground!

RUDYARD KIPLING (1865–1936)

NATURE NOTES: DANDELIONS

Incorrigible, brash,
They brightened the cinder path of my childhood,
Unsubtle, the opposite of primroses,
But, unlike primroses, capable
Of growing anywhere, railway track, pierhead,
Like our extrovert friends who never
Make us fall in love, yet fill
The primroseless roseless gaps.

MEETING

When snow lies covering the roads,
And makes the roofs its floor,
I'll start out for a walk – and see
You standing at the door;

Alone, in your autumnal coat,
Bare-haired, bootless, you stand:
You struggle with your thoughts, and chew
The damp snow in your hand.

Far out into the distant dark
Trees, fences fade away:
Alone amid the falling snow
Disconsolate you stay.

The water from your scarf rolls down
Your sleeves and lingers there:
Like morning dew the little drops
Now sparkle in your hair;

And suddenly a shining wisp
Of hair lights up your face:
It tints your scarf, your shabby coat,
Your figure's fragile grace.

The snow is wet upon your lashes,
There's anguish in your eyes,
But every feature of your face
Is a unique surprise.

As with an iron chisel
Dipped in antimony,
So clearly on my heart are you
Engraved undyingly,

And in it will for ever live
Your eyes' humility;
Be then the hard world merciless –
It has no claims on me.

And therefore this wide night of snow
Resolves itself in two:
I cannot draw the frontiers
Dividing me from you.

But who are we, and whence are we,
When of those long years' space
Only the idle words are left,
And of us not a trace?

70   BORIS PASTERNAK (1890–1960),
     TRANS. HENRY KAMEN

LA GORGUE

The long night, the short sleep, and La Gorgue
    to wander,
So be the Fates were kind and our Commander;
With a mill, and still canal, and like-Stroudway
    bridges.
One looks back on these as Time's truest riches
Which were so short an escape, so perilous a joy
Since fatigues, weather, line trouble or any
    whimsical ploy
Division might hatch out would have finished peace.

There was a house there, (I tell the noted thing)
The kindest woman kept, and an unending string
Of privates as wasps to sugar went in and out.
Friendliness sanctified all there without doubt,
As lovely as the mill above the still green
Canal where the dark fishes went almost unseen.
B Company had come down from Tilleloy
Lousy, thirsty, avid of any employ

Of peace; and this woman in leanest times had plotted
A miracle to amaze the army-witted.
And this was café-au-lait as princes know it,
And fasting, and poor-struck; dead but not to show it.
A drink of edicts, dooms, a height of tales.
Heat, cream, coffee; the maker tries and fails,
The poet too, where such thirst such mate had.
A campaign thing that makes remembrance sad.

There was light there, too, in the clear
    North French way.
It blessed the room, and bread, and the mistress giver,
The husband for his wife's sake, and both for a day
Were blessed by many soldiers tired however;
A mark in Time, a Peace, a Making-delay.

A TIME TO TALK

When a friend calls to me from the road
And slows his horse to a meaning walk,
I don't stand still and look around
On all the hills I haven't hoed,
And shout from where I am, 'What is it?'
No, not as there is a time to talk.
I thrust my hoe in the mellow ground,
Blade-end up and five feet tall,
And plod: I go up to the stone wall
For a friendly visit.

ROBERT FROST (1874–1963)

SOCIAL LIFE

THE MIXER

With a pert moustache and a ready candid smile
He has played his way through twenty years of pubs,
Deckchairs, lounges, touchlines, junctions, homes,
And still as ever popular, he roams
Far and narrow, mimicking the style
Of other people's leisure, scattering stubs.

Colourless, when alone, and self-accused,
He is only happy in reflected light
And only real in the range of laughter;
Behind his eyes are shadows of a night
In Flanders but his mind long since refused
To let that time intrude on what came after.

So in this second war which is fearful too,
He cannot away with silence but has grown
Almost a cypher, like a Latin word
That many languages have made their own
Till it is worn and blunt and easy to construe
And often spoken but no longer heard.

LOUIS MACNEICE (1907–1963)   77

OFFICE FRIENDSHIPS

Eve is madly in love with Hugh
And Hugh is keen on Jim.
Charles is in love with very few
And few are in love with him.

Myra sits typing notes of love
With romantic pianist's fingers.
Dick turns his eyes to the heavens above
Where Fran's divine perfume lingers.

Nicky is rolling eyes and tits
And flaunting her wiggly walk.
Everybody is thrilled to bits
By Clive's suggestive talk.

Sex suppressed will go berserk,
But it keeps us all alive.
It's a wonderful change from wives and work
And it ends at half past five.

SAY ABOUT SEVEN OR SEVEN-FIFTEEN

A supper party is something at which you arrive either
    long before or long after the rest of the
    competitors,
And you broke your glasses on the way over and can't
    tell people you know from people you don't know
    or your creditors from your debtitors,
And you had thought your morning shave would see
    you through and you suddenly realize that your
    chin is growing shadowy, not to say tufty,
And you discover that you are either the only male in
    evening clothes or the only one in mufti,
And as if your spirits were not by now sufficiently
    dankish,
Well, you also discover that you alone didn't know it
    was a birthday party and are the only arrival not
    to bring in a package either useful or prankish,
But with the arrival of the cocktails your spirits are
    turned from the swath and scattered for drying,
    or as the crossword puzzlers put it, tedded,
Until you realize with a shudder that you received
    through an error the cocktail specially mixed by
    the host for his brother-in-law, who is notoriously
    light-headed,

And you choke it down, and not till the salad is served
    do you recover from your croup,
At which point it seems that you have no fork left, the
    implication being either that it now rests in your
    pocket or that you used two forks on your soup.
But it is only later that the earth really begins to spin
    like a fretful midge,
When it transpires that in this gathering of eight or
    twelve or sixteen it is you and you alone by
    yourself who do not play bridge.
You may well echo the words of the poet as you
    eventually wend your homeward way.
'Fate,' said the poet firmly, 'cannot harm me further, I
    have dined today.'

THE FECKLESS DINNER-PARTY

'Who are we waiting for?' '*Soup* burnt?' '... Eight –'
  'Only the tiniest party.– Us!'
'Darling! Divine!' 'Ten minutes late –'
  'And my digest –' 'I'm *ravenous*!'
' "Toomes"?' – 'Oh, he's new,' 'Looks crazed, I guess.'
  ' "Married" – *Again!*' 'Well; more or less!'

'Dinner is *served*!' ' "Dinner is served"!'
  'Is served?' 'Is served.' 'Ah, yes.'

'Dear Mr Prout, will you take down
  The Lilith in leaf-green by the fire?
Blanche Ogleton? ...' 'How coy a frown! –
  Hasn't she borrowed *Eve's* attire?'
'Morose Old Adam!' 'Charmed – I vow.'
  'Come then, and meet her now.'

'Now, Dr. Mallus – would you please? –
  Our daring poetess, Delia Seek?'
'The lady with the bony knees?'
  'And – *entre nous* – less song than beak.'
'Sharing her past with Simple Si –'
  '*Bare* facts! He'll blush!' 'Oh, fie!'

'And *you*, Sir Nathan – false but fair! –
   That fountain of wit, Aurora Pert.'
'More wit than It, poor dear! But there . . .'
   'Pitiless Pacha! *And* such a flirt!'
' "Flirt"! *Me*?' 'Who else?' 'You here . . . Who can . . .?'
   'In*cor*rigible man!'

'And now, Mr. Simon – little me! –
   Last and –' 'By no means least!' 'Oh, come!
What naughty, naughty flattery!
   Honey! – I *hear* the creature hum!'
'Sweets for the sweet, *I* always say!'
   ' "Always"? . . . We're last.' .'*This* way?' . . .

'No, sir; straight on, please.' 'I'd have vowed! –
   I came the other . . .' 'It's queer; I'm sure . . .'
'What frightful pictures!' 'Fiends!' 'The *crowd*!'
   'Such nudes!' 'I can't endure . . .'

'Yes, *there* they go.' 'Heavens! *Are* we right?'
   'Follow up closer!' ' "Prout"? – sand-blind!'
'This endless . . .' 'Who's turned down the light?'
   'Keep calm! They're close behind.'

'Oh! Dr. Mallus; what dismal stairs!
   I hate these old Victor . . .' 'Dry rot!'

'Darker and darker!' 'Fog!' 'The air's ...'
  'Scarce breathable!' 'Hell!' '*What*?'

'The banister's gone!' 'It's deep; keep close!'
  'We're going down and down!' 'What fun!'
'Damp! Why, my shoes ...' 'It's slimy ... Not *moss*!'
  'I'm freezing cold!' 'Let's run.'

'... Behind us. I'm giddy ...' 'The catacombs ...'
  'That shout!' 'Who's there?' 'I'm *alone*!' 'Stand back!'
'She said, Lead ...' 'Oh!' 'Where's Toomes?' '*Toomes*!'
    'Toomes!'
  'Stifling!' 'My skull will crack!'

'Sir Nathan! *Ai*!' 'I *say*! *Toomes*! Prout!'
  'Where? Where?' ' "Our silks and fine array" ...'
'She's mad.' 'I'm dying!' 'Oh, let me *out*!'
  'My God! We've lost our way!' ...

And now how sad-serene the abandoned house
Whereon at dawn the spring-tide sunbeams beat;
And time's slow pace alone is ominous,
And naught but shadows of noonday therein meet;
Domestic microcosm, only a Trump could rouse:
And, pondering darkly, in the silent rooms,
He who misled them all – the butler, Toomes.

WALTER DE LA MARE (1873–1956)   83

INVITING A FRIEND TO SUPPER

Tonight, grave sir, both my poor house and I
    Do equally desire your company;
Not that we think us worthy such a guest,
    But that your worth will dignify our feast
With those that come; whose grace may make that
      seem
    Something, which else could hope for no esteem.
It is the fair acceptance, sir, creates
    The entertainment perfect, not the cates.
Yet shall you have, to rectify your palate,
    An olive, capers, or some better salad
Ushering the mutton; with a short-legged hen,
    If we can get her, full of eggs, and then
Lemons, and wine for sauce; to these, a coney
    Is not to be despaired of, for our money;
And though fowl now be scarce, yet there are clerks,
    The sky not falling, think we may have larks.
I'll tell you of more, and lie, so you will come:
    Of partridge, pheasant, woodcock, of which some
May yet be there; and godwit, if we can;
    Knat, rail and ruff, too. Howsoe'er, my man
Shall read a piece of Virgil, Tacitus,
    Livy, or of some better book to us,
Of which we'll speak our minds, amidst our meat;
    And I'll profess no verses to repeat;

To this, if aught appear which I not know of,
    That will the pastry, not my paper, show of.
Digestive cheese and fruit there sure will be;
    But that which most doth take my muse and me
Is a pure cup of rich Canary wine,
    Which is the Mermaid's now, but shall be mine;
Of which had Horace or Anacreon tasted,
    Their lives, as do their lines, till now had lasted.
Tobacco, nectar, or the Thespian spring
    Are all but Luther's beer to this I sing.
Of this we will sup free, but moderately;
    And we will have no Poley or Parrot by;
Nor shall our cups make any guilty men,
    But at our parting we will be as when
We innocently met. No simple word
    That shall be uttered at our mirthful board
Shall make us sad next morning, or affright
    The liberty that we'll enjoy tonight.

BEN JONSON (1572/3–1637)   85

ODE TO BEN JONSON

Ah *Ben*!
Say how, or when
Shall we thy Guests
Meet at those *Lyrick* Feasts,
Made at the *Sun*,
The *Dog*, the triple *Tunne*?
Where we such clusters had,
As made us nobly wild, not mad;
And yet each Verse of thine
Out-did the meate, out-did the frolick wine.

My *Ben*
Or come agen,
Or send to us
Thy wit's great over-plus;
But teach us yet
Wisely to husband it;
Lest we that Talent spend:
And having once brought to an end
That precious stock, the store
Of such a wit the world should have no more.

OF FRIENDSHIP

Choose judiciously thy friends; for to discard them
    is undesirable,
Yet it is better to drop thy friends, O my daughter,
    than to drop thy H's.
Dost thou know a wise woman? yea, wiser than
    the children of light?
Hath she a position? and a title? and are her parties
    in the Morning Post?
If thou dost, cleave unto her, and give up unto her
    thy body and mind;
Think with her ideas, and distribute thy smiles at her
    bidding:
So shalt thou become like unto her; and thy manners
    shall be "formed,"
And thy name shall be a Sesame, at which the doors
    of the great shall fly open:
Thou shalt know every Peer, his arms, and the date
    of his creation,
His pedigree and their intermarriages, and cousins
    to the sixth remove:
Thou shalt kiss the hand of Royalty, and lo!
    in next morning's papers,

Side by side with rumours of wars, and stories
        of shipwrecks and sieges,
Shall appear thy name, and the minutiæ of
        thy head-dress and petticoat,
For an enraptured public to muse upon
        over their matutinal muffin.

VERS DE SOCIÉTÉ

My wife and I have asked a crowd of craps
To come and waste their time and ours: perhaps
You'd care to join us? In a pig's arse, friend.
Day comes to an end.
The gas fire breathes, the trees are darkly swayed.
And so *Dear Warlock-Williams: I'm afraid* —

Funny how hard it is to be alone.
I could spend half my evenings, if I wanted,
Holding a glass of washing sherry, canted
Over to catch the drivel of some bitch
Who's read nothing but *Which*;
Just think of all the spare time that has flown

Straight into nothingness by being filled
With forks and faces, rather than repaid
Under a lamp, hearing the noise of wind,
And looking out to see the moon thinned
To an air-sharpened blade.
A life, and yet how sternly it's instilled

All solitude is selfish. No one now
Believes the hermit with his gown and dish
Talking to God (who's gone too); the big wish
Is to have people nice to you, which means
Doing it back somehow.
Virtue is social. Are, then, these routines

Playing at goodness, like going to church?
Something that bores us, something we don't do well
(Asking that ass about his fool research)
But try to feel, because, however crudely,
It shows us what should be?
Too subtle, that. Too decent, too. Oh hell,

Only the young can be alone freely.
The time is shorter now for company,
And sitting by a lamp more often brings
Not peace, but other things.
Beyond the light stand failure and remorse
Whispering *Dear Warlock-Williams: Why, of course* –

LAST NIGHT, AFTER FIVE
PINTS OF WINE

Last night, after five pints of wine,
I said, 'Procillus, come and dine
Tomorrow.' You assumed I meant
What I said (a dangerous precedent)
And slyly jotted down a note
Of my drunk offer. Let me quote
A proverb from the Greek: 'I hate
an unforgetful drinking mate'.

IN THE GARDEN

A mild parochial talk was ours;
The air of afternoon was sweet
With burthen of the sun-parched flowers;
His fiery beams in fury beat
From out the O of space, and made,
Wherever leaves his glare let through,
Circlets of brilliance in the shade
Of his unfathomable blue.

Old Dr. Salmon sat pensive and grey,
And Archie's tongue was never still,
While dear Miss Arbuthnot fanned away
The stress of walking up the hill.
And little Bertha? – how bony a cheek!
How ghast an eye! Poor mite . . . That pause –
When not even tactful tongues could speak! . . .
The drowsy Cat pushed out her claws.

A bland, unvexing talk was ours –
Sharing that gentle gilded cage –
Manners and morals its two brief hours
Proffered alike to youth and age.
Why break so pleasing a truce? – forfend!
Why on such sweetness and light intrude?
Why bid the child, 'Cough, "*Ah!*" ' – and end
Our complaisance; her solitude?

LEAVING

As we left the garden-party
By the far gate,
There were many loitering on
Who had come late

And a few arriving still,
Though the lawn lay
Like a fast-draining shoal
Of ochre day.

Curt shadows in the grass
Hatched every blade,
And now on pedestals
Of mounting shade

Stood all our friends – iconic,
Now, in mien,
Half-lost in dignities
Till now unseen.

There were the hostess' hands
Held out to greet
The scholar's limp, his wife's
Quick-pecking feet.

And there was wit's cocked head,
And there the sleek
And gaze-enameled look
Of beauty's cheek.

We saw now, loitering there
Knee-deep in night,
How even the wheeling children
Moved in a rite

Or masque, or long charade
Where we, like these,
Had blundered into grand
Identities,

Filling our selves as sculpture
Fills the stone.
We had not played so surely,
Had we known.

DUMB FRIENDS

FREDERICK KUH, MANX CAT
for Jean Stafford

Closer to us than most of our close friends,
the only friend we never quarrelled over,
the sole survivor of our first marriage, I see him
on catnip, bobtailed, bobbing like a rabbit,
streaking up the slender wand of a tree,
scratching the polished bark and glassy sprouts,
preferring to hang hooked than lift a claw.
Windtoy, Lynxears, Furfall, you had eyes,
you lowered yourself to us, clockclaw, clickclaw –
to where no one backed down or lost a point.
Cats aren't quite lost despite too many lives.
Which of us will ever manage one,
or storm the heights and gracefully back down –
Jean, those years multiplied beyond subtraction?

From JUBILATE AGNO

For I will consider my Cat Jeoffry.

For he is the servant of the Living God, duly and daily
      serving him ...

For his tongue is exceeding pure so that it has in purity
      what it wants in music.

For he is docile and can learn certain things.

For he can sit up with gravity, which is patience upon
      approbation.

For he can fetch and carry, which is patience in
      employment.

For he can jump over a stick, which is patience upon
      proof positive.

For he can spraggle upon waggle at the word of
      command.

For he can jump from an eminence into his
      master's bosom.

For he can catch the cork and toss it again.

For he is hated by the hypocrite and miser.

For the former is afraid of detection.

For the latter refuses the charge.

For he camels his back to bear the first notion of
      business.

For he is good to think on, if a man would express
      himself neatly.

For he made a great figure in Egypt
    for his signal services.
For he killed the Icneumon rat, very pernicious
    by land.
For his ears are so acute that they sting again.
For from this proceeds the passing quickness
    of his attention.
For by stroking of him I have found out electricity.
For I perceived God's light about him both wax and
    fire.
For the electrical fire is the spiritual substance which
    God sends from heaven to sustain the bodies
    both of man and beast.
For God has blessed him in the variety
    of his movements.
For, though he cannot fly, he is an excellent clamberer.
For his motions upon the face of the earth are more
    than any other quadruped.
For he can tread to all the measures upon the music.
For he can swim for life.
For he can creep.

LAST WORDS TO A DUMB FRIEND

Pet was never mourned as you,
Purrer of the spotless hue,
Plumy tail, and wistful gaze
While you humoured our queer ways,
Or outshrilled your morning call
Up the stairs and through the hall –
Foot suspended in its fall –
While, expectant, you would stand
Arched, to meet the stroking hand;
Till your way you chose to wend
Yonder, to your tragic end.

Never another pet for me!
Let your place all vacant be;
Better blankness day by day
Than companion torn away.
Better bid his memory fade,
Better blot each mark he made,
Selfishly escape distress
By contrived forgetfulness,
Than preserve his prints to make
Every morn and eve an ache.

From the chair wheron he sat
Sweep his fur, nor wince thereat;
Rake his little pathways out
Mid the bushes roundabout;
Smooth away his talons' mark
From the claw-worn pine-tree bark,
Where he climbed as dusk embrowned,
Waiting us who loitered round.

Strange it is this speechless thing,
Subject to our mastering,
Subject for his life and food
To our gift, and time, and mood;
Timid pensioner of us Powers,
His existence ruled by ours,
Should – by crossing at a breath
Into safe and shielded death,
By the merely taking hence
Of his insignificance –
Loom as largened to the sense,
Shape as part, above man's will,
Of the Imperturbable.

As a prisoner, flight debarred,
Exercising in a yard,
Still retain I, troubled, shaken,
Mean estate, by him forsaken;
And this home, which scarcely took
Impress from his little look,
By his faring to the Dim
Grows all eloquent of him.

Housemate, I can think you still
Bounding to the window-sill,
Over which I vaguely see
Your small mound beneath the tree,
Showing in the autumn shade
That you moulder where you played.

FLUSH OR FAUNUS

You see this dog; it was but yesterday
I mused forgetful of his presence here,
Till thought on thought drew downward tear on tear:
When from the pillow where wet-cheeked I lay,
A head as hairy as Faunus thrust its way
Right sudden against my face, two golden-clear
Great eyes astonished mine, a drooping ear
Did flap me on either cheek to dry the spray!
I started first as some Arcadian
Amazed by goatly god in twilight grove:
But as the bearded vision closelier ran
My tears off, I knew Flush, and rose above
Surprise and sadness, – thanking the true PAN
Who by low creatures leads to heights of love.

BOUNCE TO POPE

Master, by Styx! – which is the poets' oath,
And the dread bourne of dogs and poets both –
Dear Master, destined soon my fate to share,
'Twas not for want of meat or love, I swear,
Bounce left thee early for the Stygian shore:
I went ('twas all I could) to be before;
To wait, as oft in life, when thou wouldst roam,
I watched to have thy greeting coming home.
So here I prick my ears and strain to mark
Thy slight form coming after through the dark,
And leap to meet thee; with my deep bark drown
Thy: 'Bounce! why Bounce, old friend! nay, down,
        Bounce, down!'
Then, master, shall I turn and, at thy side,
Pace till we reach the river's foetid tide.
The monstrous shapes and terrors of the way
Shall flee, themselves in terror, at my bay;
Gorgons, chimaeras, hydras at my growl
Scatter, and harpies prove pacific fowl;
Charon shall give prompt passage; what is more,
Seem civil till we reach the farther shore;
And last – for this is dog's work – at the Gate
where the three-headed Cerberus lies in wait,
Thou shalt not need or lyre or hydromel
To mollify the gruesome Hound of Hell

But may'st pass through unscath'd: he will not mind
Seeing with thee, a female of his kind.

There must I leave thee; there to feel thy hand
Bestow a final pat, great Bounce shall stand,
Knowing, alas, that I may do no more
Than gaze and grieve and, while I can, adore.
Watching thy cheerful, firm, unhurried tread
Down that long road declining to the dead,
And think, to see that dwindling shade depart:
'So small a master, but how great a heart!'

ARGUS

When wise Ulysses from his native Coast
Long kept by Wars, and long by Tempests tost,
Arriv'd at last, poor, old, disguis'd, alone,
To all his Friends & ev'n his Queen unknown,
Chang'd as he was, with Age, & Toils, & Cares,
Furrowd his rev'rend Face, & white his hairs,
In his own Palace forc'd to ask his Bread,
Scorn'd by those Slaves his former Bounty fed,
Forgot of all his own Domestic Crew;
His faithful Dog his rightful Master knew!
Unfed, unhousd, neglected, on the Clay,
Like an old Servant, now cashier'd, he lay,
And tho' ev'n then expiring on the Plain,
Touch'd with Resentment of ungrateful Man,
And longing to behold his Ancient Lord again.
Him when he Saw – he rose, & crawld to meet,
(Twas all he cou'd) and fawn'd, and kist his feet,
Seiz'd with dumb Joy – then falling by his Side,
Own'd his returning Lord, Look'd up, & Dy'd.

THE PARDON

My dog lay dead five days without a grave
In the thick of summer, hid in a clump of pine
And a jungle of grass and honeysuckle-vine.
I who had loved him while he kept alive

Went only close enough to where he was
To sniff the heavy honeysuckle-smell
Twined with another odor heavier still
And hear the flies' intolerable buzz.

Well, I was ten and very much afraid.
In my kind world the dead were out of range
And I could not forgive the sad or strange
In beast or man. My father took the spade

And buried him. Last night I saw the grass
Slowly divide (it was the same scene
But now it glowed a fierce and mortal green)
And saw the dog emerging. I confess

I felt afraid again, but still he came
In the carnal sun, clothed in a hymn of flies,
And death was breeding in his lively eyes.
I started in to cry and call his name,

Asking forgiveness of his tongueless head.
... I dreamt the past was never past redeeming:
But whether this was false or honest dreaming
I beg death's pardon now. And mourn the dead.

AN EPITAPH

His friends he loved. His direst earthly foes –
    Cats – I believe he did but feign to hate.
My hand will miss the insinuated nose,
    Mine eyes the tail that wagg'd contempt at Fate.

WILLIAM WATSON (1858–1935)

EPITAPH OF A DOG

Stranger by the roadside, do not smile
When you see this grave, though it is only a dog's.
My master wept when I died, and his own hand
Laid me in earth and wrote these lines on my tomb.

ANON, TRANS. DUDLEY FITTS

MY PET HARE
From THE TASK, III

Well – one at least is safe. One shelter'd hare
Has never heard the sanguinary yell
Of cruel man, exulting in her woes.
Innocent partner of my peaceful home,
Whom ten long years' experience of my care
Has made at last familiar; she has lost
Much of her vigilant instinctive dread,
Not needful here, beneath a roof like mine.
Yes – thou mayst eat thy bread, and lick the hand
That feeds thee; thou mayst frolic on the floor
At evening, and at night retire secure
To thy straw couch, and slumber unalarm'd;
For I have gain'd thy confidence, have pledged
All that is human in me, to protect
Thine unsuspecting gratitude and love.
If I survive thee, I will dig thy grave;
And, when I place thee in it, sighing say,
I knew at least one hare that had a friend.

From PHILIP SPARROW

It had a velvet cap,
And would sit upon my lap,
And seek after small wormès,
And sometime white bread-crumbès;
And many times and oft
Between my breastès soft
It wouldè lie and rest;
It was proper and prest.

Sometime he would gasp
When he saw a wasp;
A fly or a gnat,
He would fly at that;
And prettily he would pant
When he saw an ant,
Lord, how he would pry
After the butterfly!
Lord, how he would hop
After the gressop!
And when I said, 'Phip, Phip!'
Then he would leap and skip,
And take me by the lip.
Alas, it will me slo
That Philip is gone me fro! . . .

For it would come and go,
And fly so to and fro;
And on me it wouldè leap
When I was asleep,
And his feathers shake,
Wherewith he wouldè make
Me often for to wake,
And for to take him in
Upon my naked skin.
God wot, we thought no sin;
What though he crept so low?
It was no hurt, I trow
He did nothing, perdè,
But sit upon my knee.
Philip, though he were nice,
In him it was no vice.
Philip had leave to go
To peck my little toe;
Philip might be bold
And do what he wold:
Philip would seek and take
All the fleas black
That he could there espy
With his wanton eye.

LUX, MY FAIR FALCON

Lux, my fair falcon, and your fellows all,
    How well pleasaunt it were your liberty!
Ye not forsake me that fair might ye befall.
    But they that sometime lik'd my company,
Like lice away from dead bodies they crawl:
    Lo, what a proof in light adversity!
But ye, my birds, I swear by all your bells,
Ye be my friends, and so be but few else.

PARTRIDGE

Never, my partridge, O patient heart,
Were you to see your hills again.
And never now will you wake up
In your elegant wicker coop,
Shake as the fat-eyed day comes on,
And freckle your wings with the dawn.
The greedy cat has got your head,
I've taken what's left from her teeth
And hidden you well from her claws.
Small bodies should not lie so deep.
May the dust be light on your grave.

GOOD-NIGHT

The skylarks are far behind that sang over the down;
I can hear no more those suburb nightingales;
Thrushes and blackbirds sing in the gardens of the
     town
In vain: the noise of man, beast, and machine prevails.

But the call of children in the unfamiliar streets
That echo with a familiar twilight echoing,
Sweet as the voice of nightingale or lark, completes
A magic of strange welcome, so that I seem a king

Among man, beast, machine, bird, child, and the ghost
That in the echo lives and with the echo dies.
The friendless town is friendly; homeless, I am not
     lost;
Though I know none of these doors, and meet but
     strangers' eyes.

Never again, perhaps, after tomorrow, shall
I see these homely streets, these church windows
     alight,
Not a man or woman or child among them all:
But it is All Friends' Night, a traveller's good night.

EDWARD THOMAS (1878–1917)   117

A DUMB FRIEND

I planted a young tree when I was young:
But now the tree is grown and I am old:
There wintry robin shelters from the cold
    And tunes his silver tongue.

A green and living tree I planted it,
A glossy-foliaged tree of evergreen:
All through the noontide heat it spread a screen
    Whereunder I might sit.

But now I only watch it where it towers:
I, sitting at my window, watch it tost
By rattling gale or silvered by the frost;
    Or, when sweet summer flowers,

Wagging its round green head with stately grace
In tender winds that kiss it and go by.
It shows a green full age: and what show I?
    A faded wrinkled face.

So often have I watched it, till mine eyes
Have filled with tears and I have ceased to see,
That now it seems a very friend to me,
    In all my secrets wise.

A faithful pleasant friend, who year by year
Grew with my growth and strengthened with my
        strength,
But whose green lifetime shows a longer length;
        When I shall not sit here

It still will bud in spring, and shed rare leaves
In autumn, and in summer-heat give shade,
And warmth in winter: when my bed is made
        In shade the cypress weaves.

From DESK

My desk, most loyal friend
   thank you. You've been with me on
every road I've taken.
   My scar and my protection.

My loaded writing mule.
   Your tough legs have endured
the weight of all my dreams, and
   burdens of piled-up thoughts.

Thank you   for toughening me.
   No worldly joy could pass
your severe looking-glass
   you blocked the first temptation,

and every base desire
   your heavy oak outweighed
lions of hate, elephants
   of spite   you intercepted.

Thank you for growing with me
   as my need grew in size
I've been laid out across you
   so many years   alive ...

I celebrate thirty years
    of union   truer than love
I know every notch in your wood.
    You know the lines in my face.

Haven't you written them there?
    devouring reams of paper
denying me any tomorrow
    teaching me only today.

You've thrown my important letters
    and money   in floods together,
repeating: for every single verse
    today has to be the deadline.

You've warned me of retribution
    not to be measured in spoonfuls.
And when   my body will be laid out,
    Great fool! Let it be on you then.

MARINA TSVETAYEVA (1892–1941),   121
TRANS. ELAINE FEINSTEIN

TOBACCO PLANT

We wondered at the tobacco plants there in France
And hung on the rafters brown where our bacon hangs
Sunny in the clear light autumn wind a-dance;
Or to be looked at upwards in its dry ranks,
But the wonder more when in cold nights fumes arose
From the hidden bags, and the frost
     a moment grew less.

'What! you love smoking, indeed?' he said, and I
Spoke with love of Virginia and Egypt, but not a
Good word for tobacco issue wherever given
And the talk passed to my love
     of the dear French heaven,
Her people, her soldiers, her books,
     music and lovely land.
Speaking broken French he could
     hardly easily understand,
Until I spoke of Daudet, whose book I loved
And of Ronsard, Molière, others,
     the *Journals* that proved
Friendly enough in that news-lacking and forlorn land.
Talking of all my love, all, in forlorn exile.

Till, looking up in the comfort of that fire-warm room
I saw the tobacco plants – brown leaves on the beams
Reminding gratitude of tobacco's never-ending boon,
Happy to see the leaf, after the smoked thing in gleams
Whirling white puffs contented to the ceiling's gloom.
And thank the gods for one thing
        in these damned extremes,
And his man's friendliness so good to have,
        and lost so soon.

PORTRAITS

BY WAY OF PREFACE

'How pleasant to know Mr. Lear!'
    Who has written such volumes of stuff!
Some think him ill-tempered and queer,
    But a few think him pleasant enough.

His mind is concrete and fastidious,
    His nose is remarkably big;
His visage is more or less hideous,
    His beard it resembles a wig.

He has ears, and two eyes, and ten fingers,
    Leastways if you reckon two thumbs;
Long ago he was one of the singers,
    But now he is one of the dumbs.

He sits in a beautiful parlour,
    With hundreds of books on the wall;
He drinks a great deal of Marsala,
    But never gets tipsy at all.

He has many friends, laymen and clerical,
    Old Foss is the name of his cat;
His body is perfectly spherical,
    He weareth a runcible hat.

When he walks in a waterproof white,
    The children run after him so!
Calling out, 'He's come out in his night-
    gown, that crazy old Englishman, oh!'

He weeps by the side of the ocean,
    He weeps on the top of the hill;
He purchases pancakes and lotion,
    And chocolate shrimps from the mill.

He reads but he cannot speak Spanish,
    He cannot abide ginger-beer:
Ere the days of his pilgrimage vanish,
    How pleasant to know Mr. Lear!

FRIENDS

Now must I these three praise –
Three women that have wrought
What joy is in my days:
One because no thought,
Nor those unpassing cares,
No, not in these fifteen
Many-times-troubled years,
Could ever come between
Mind and delighted mind;
And one because her hand
Had strength that could unbind
What none can understand,
What none can have and thrive,
Youth's dreamy load, till she
So changed me that I live
Labouring in ecstasy.
And what of her that took
All till my youth was gone
With scarce a pitying look?
How could I praise that one?

When day begins to break
I count my good and bad,
Being wakeful for her sake,
Remembering what she had,
What eagle look still shows,
While up from my heart's root
So great a sweetness flows
I shake from head to foot.

A LETTER FROM BROOKLYN

An old lady writes me in a spidery style,
Each character trembling, and I see a veined hand
Pellucid as paper, travelling on a skein
Of such frail thoughts its thread is often broken;
Or else the filament from which a phrase is hung
Dims to my sense, but caught, it shines like steel,
As touch a line and the whole web will feel.
She describes my father, yet I forget her face
More easily than my father's yearly dying;
Of her I remember small, buttoned boots and the place
She kept in our wooden church on those Sundays
Whenever her strength allowed;
Grey-haired, thin-voiced, perpetually bowed.

'I am Mable Rawlins,' she writes,
      'and know both your parents';
He is dead, Miss Rawlins, but God bless your tense:
'Your father was a dutiful, honest,
Faithful, and useful person.'
For such plain praise what fame is recompense?
'A horn-painter, he painted delicately on horn,
He used to sit around the table and paint pictures.'
The peace of God needs nothing to adorn
It, nor glory nor ambition.

'He is twenty-eight years buried,' she writes,
    'he was called home,
And is, I am sure, doing greater work.'

The strength of one frail hand in a dim room
Somewhere in Brooklyn, patient and assured,
Restores my sacred duty to the Word.
'Home, home,' she can write
    with such short time to live,
Alone as she spins the blessings of her years;
Not withered of beauty if she can bring such tears,
Nor withdrawn from the world
    that breaks its lovers so;
Heaven is to her the place where painters go,
All who bring beauty on frail shell or horn,
There was all made, thence their *lux-mundi* drawn,
Drawn, drawn, till the thread is resilient steel,
Lost though it seems in darkening periods,
And there they return to do work that is God's.

So this old lady writes, and again I believe.
I believe it all, and for no man's death I grieve.

HEARING THAT HIS FRIEND
WAS COMING BACK FROM THE WAR

In old days those who went to fight
In three years had one year's leave.
But in *this* war the soldiers are never changed;
They must go on fighting till they die
    on the battlefield.
I thought of you, so weak and indolent,
Hopelessly trying to learn to march and drill.
That a young man should ever come home again
Seemed about as likely as that the sky should fall.
Since I got the news that you were coming back,
Twice I have mounted to the high wall of your home.
I found your brother mending your horse's stall;
I found your mother sewing your new clothes.
I am half afraid; perhaps it is not true;
Yet I never weary of watching for you on the road.
Each day I go out at the City Gate
With a flask of wine, lest you should come thirsty.
Oh that I could shrink the surface of the World,
So that suddenly I might find you standing at my side!

WANG CHIEN (AD *c.* 756–835)   133

TOWNSHEND

Townshend? I knew him well, queer ways he had.
Fond of plays, fond of books, and of Roman talk,
Campments, marches, *pila*, and a mix of relics
Found by western folk in a casual walk.
A quick man in his talk, with eyes always sad.
Kind? Yes, and honourer of poets and actor folk.
Chettle and Heywood ... but most Jonson he loved.
Angry with London for neglect that so evil proved
Who lived two years with him and was great labourer
As 'Cataline' and many other things to which
    he was moved
Showed; he read much Latin, and was proud of Greek.
Townshend would leave him whole days alone
    in his house
And go to Surrey or Buckingham and take delight,
Or watch Danbury changing in the March light,
Knowing Jonson labouring like the great son he was
Of Solway and of Westminster – O, maker, maker,
Given of all the gods to anything but grace.
And kind as all the apprentices knew and scholars;
A talker with battle honours till dawn whitened
    the curtains,
With many honourers, and many many enemies,
    and followers.

There's one said to me 'I love his face,
But if he smites me flat for a false Greek quantity,
And drinks a quart where I should be trembler
    and shaker,
It must be said, "I love him". He does me disgrace
And I shall pay him back for the sight of posterity
For all great "Cataline" and "Alchemist" its high play,
Unless he loves me more or I have greater charity.'

POETS TOGETHER

TO A FRIEND

If it be true that poets, as you say,
Envisage in their verse and populate,
By dreams that shall come true, the future state,
I must be careful whom I shall portray
Lest I sit down, forever and for aye,
With the strange characters I celebrate.
O awful thought: our Fancy is our Fate!
(Let me erase some writings while I may!)
But one thing I am sure of, dear A.E.:
I will confront the malcreated crew,
Victims or merely subjects of my song,
If I can reach the bourne where you shall be
Creating kindness as you always do,
And I may bring my fancy friends along.

OLIVER ST JOHN GOGARTY (1878–1957)   139

From AN EPISTLE TO DR ARBUTHNOT

There are, who to my person pay their court:
I cough like Horace, and though lean, am short,
Ammon's great son one shoulder had too high,
Such Ovid's nose, and 'Sir! you have an eye' –
Go on, obliging creatures, make me see
All that disgraced my betters, met in me.
Say for my comfort, languishing in bed,
'Just so immortal Maro held his head':
And when I die be sure you let me know
Great Homer died three thousand years ago.

Why did I write? what sin to me unknown
Dipped me in ink, my parents' or my own?
As yet a child, nor yet a fool to fame,
I lisped in numbers, for the numbers came.
I left no calling for this idle trade,
No duty broke, no father disobeyed.
The Muse but served to ease some friend, not wife,
To help me through this long disease, my life,
To second, ARBUTHNOT! thy art and care,
And teach the being you preserved, to bear.

But why then publish? Granville the polite,
And knowing Walsh, would tell me I could write;
Well-natured Garth inflamed with early praise;
And Congreve loved, and Swift endured my lays;
The courtly Talbot, Somers, Sheffield read,

Even mitred Rochester would nod the head,
And St John's self (great Dryden's friends before)
With open arms received one poet more.
Happy my studies, when by these approved!
Happier their author, when by these beloved!

TO E. T.

I slumbered with your poems on my breast
Spread open as I dropped them half-read through
Like dove wings on a figure on a tomb
To see, if in a dream they brought of you,

I might not have the chance I missed in life
Through some delay, and call you to your face
First soldier, and then poet, and then both,
Who died a soldier-poet of your race.

I meant, you meant, that nothing should remain
Unsaid between us, brother, and this remained –
And one thing more that was not then to say:
The Victory for what it lost and gained.

You went to meet the shell's embrace of fire
On Vimy Ridge; and when you fell that day
The war seemed over more for you than me,
But now for me than you – the other way.

How over, though, for even me who knew
The foe thrust back unsafe beyond the Rhine,
If I was not to speak of it to you
And see you pleased once more with words of mine?

142   ROBERT FROST (1874–1963)

TO E. FITZGERALD

Old Fitz, who from your suburb grange,
   Where once I tarried for a while,
Glance at the wheeling Orb of change,
   And greet it with a kindly smile;
Whom yet I see as there you sit
   Beneath your sheltering garden-tree,
And while your doves about you flit,
   And plant on shoulder, hand and knee,
Or on your head their rosy feet ...
                 but none can say
That Lenten fare makes Lenten thought,
   Who reads your golden Eastern lay,
Than which I know no version done
   In English more divinely well;
A planet equal to the sun
   Which cast it, that large infidel
Your Omar; and your Omar drew
   Full-handed plaudits from our best
In modern letters, and from two,
   Old friends outvaluing all the rest,
Two voices heard on earth no more;
   But we old friends are still alive,
And I am nearing seventy-four,
   While you have touched at seventy-five,

And so I send a birthday line
    Of greeting; and my son, who dipt
In some forgotten book of mine
    With sallow scraps of manuscript,
And dating many a year ago,
    Has hit on this, which you will take
My Fitz, and welcome, as I know
    Less for its own than for the sake
Of one recalling gracious times,
    When, in our younger London days,
You found some merit in my rhymes,
    And I more pleasure in your praise.

SUPPER WITH LINDSAY

I deal in wisdom, not in dry desire.
Luck! Luck! that's what I care for in a cage
And what fool wouldn't, when things from sleep
Come easy to the sill, things lost from far away.
Behold, the Moon! –
And it stepped in the room, under his arm, –
Lindsay's I mean: two moons, or even three,
I'd say my face is just as round as his,
And that makes three, counting his face as one.
'What Moon?' he cried, half-turning in mock fury.

And then it spilled:
The sudden light spilled on the floor like cream
From a knocked over churn, and foamed around
Us, under the chair-rungs, toward the cellar door.

'Let's eat!' said Lindsay. 'Here we've got the Moon,
We've got the living light, but where's the food?'

'Sure, we still eat,' I said. 'Enough! Or too much.'
– 'That means Blake, too?'

　　　　　　　When Lindsay bent his head
Half sideways in the shifting light,
His nose looked even bigger than it was,
And one eye gazed askew. 'Why, Blake, he's dead, –
But come to think, they say the same of me.'

When he said that, a spidery shape dropped down
A swaying light-cord, then ran half-way back.

'That's never Blake,' said Lindsay. 'He'd be a worm,
One of those fat ones winding through a rose.
Maybe it's Whitman's spider, I can't tell,
Let's eat before the moonlight all runs out.'

TO DELMORE SCHWARTZ
Cambridge 1946

We couldn't even keep the furnace lit!
Even when we had disconnected it,
the antiquated
refrigerator gurgled mustard gas
through your mustard-yellow house,
and spoiled our long maneuvred visit
from T. S. Eliot's brother, Henry Ware ...

Your stuffed duck craned toward Harvard from my
          trunk:
its bill was a black whistle, and its brow
was high and thinner than a baby's thumb,
its webs were tough as toenails on its bough.
It was your first kill, you had rushed it home,
pickled in a tin wastebasket of rum –
it looked through us, as if it'd died dead drunk.
You must have propped its eyelids with a nail,
and yet it lived with us and met our stare,
Rabelaisian, lubricious, drugged. And there,
perched on my trunk and typing-table,
it cooled our universal
Angst a moment, Delmore. We drank and eyed
the chicken-hearted shadows of the world.
Underseas fellows, nobly mad,

we talked away our friends. 'Let Joyce and Freud,
the Masters of Joy,
be our guests here,' you said. The room was filled
with cigarette smoke circling the paranoid,
inert gaze of Coleridge, back
from Malta – his eyes lost in flesh, lips baked and black.
Your tiger kitten, *Oranges*,
cartwheeled for joy in a ball of snarls.
You said:
'We poets in our youth begin in sadness;
thereof in the end come despondency and madness;
Stalin has had two cerebral hemorrhages!'
The Charles
River was turning silver. In the ebb-
light of morning, we stuck
the duck
-'s web-
foot, like a candle, in a quart of gin we'd killed.

THE SUN USED TO SHINE

The sun used to shine while we two walked
Slowly together, paused and started
Again, and sometimes mused, sometimes talked
As either pleased, and cheerfully parted

Each night. We never disagreed
Which gate to rest on. The to be
And the late past we gave small heed.
We turned from men or poetry

To rumours of the war remote
Only till both stood disinclined
For aught but the yellow flavorous coat
Of an apple wasps had undermined;

Or a sentry of dark betonies,
The stateliest of small flowers on earth,
At the forest verge; or crocuses
Pale purple as if they had their birth

In sunless Hades fields. The war
Came back to mind with the moonrise
Which soldiers in the east afar
Beheld then. Nevertheless, our eyes

Could as well imagine the Crusades
Or Caesar's battles. Everything
To faintness like those rumours fades –
Like the brook's water glittering

Under the moonlight – like those walks
Now – like us two that took them, and
The fallen apples, all the talks
And silences – like memory's sand

When the tide covers it late or soon,
And other men through other flowers
In those fields under the same moon
Go talking and have easy hours.

THIS LIFE ON EARTH'S A POISON TREE

This life on earth's a poison tree,
And yet with two fruits sweet:
Ambrosia of poesy,
And joy when true friends meet.

KÂLIDÂSA (?3RD CENTURY AD),   151
TRANS. JOHN BROUGH

TO MRS M. A. AT PARTING

I have examin'd and do find,
    Of all that favour me,
There's none I grieve to leave behind
    But only, only thee.
To part with thee I needs must die,
Could parting sep'rate thee and I.

But neither Chance nor Compliment
    Did element our Love;
'Twas sacred Sympathy was lent
    Us from the quire above.
That Friendship Fortune did create,
Still fears a wound from Time or Fate.

Our chang'd and mingled souls are grown
    To such acquaintance now,
That if each would resume their own,
    Alas! we know not how.
We have each other so engrost,
That each is in the union lost.

And thus we can no Absence know,
    Nor shall we be confin'd;
Our active souls will daily go
    To learn each other's mind.
Nay, should we never meet to Sense,
Our souls would hold Intelligence.

Inspired with a flame divine,
    I scorn to court a stay;
For from that noble soul of thine
    I ne'er can be away.
But I shall weep when thou dost grieve;
Nor can I die whilst thou dost live.

By my own temper I shall guess
    At thy felicity,
And only like my happiness
    Because it pleaseth thee.
Our hearts at any time will tell,
If thou, or I be sick, or well.

All Honour sure I must pretend,
    All that is good or Great;
She that would be Rosania's Friend,
    Must be at least complete.
If I have any bravery,
'Tis cause I have so much of thee.

Thy lieger soul in me shall lie,
    And all thy thoughts reveal;
Then back again with mine shall fly,
    And thence to me shall steal.
Thus still to one another tend;
Such is the sacred Name of Friend.

Thus our twin-souls in one shall grow,
    And teach the World new love,
Redeem the age and sex, and show
    A flame Fate dares not move:
And courting Death to be our friend,
Our lives together too shall end.

A dew shall dwell upon our Tomb
    Of such a quality,
That fighting armies, thither come,
    Shall reconcilèd be.
We'll ask no Epitaph, but say
    ORINDA and ROSANIA.

FOR JOHN BERRYMAN
(*After reading his last* Dream Song)

The last years we only met
when you were on the road,
and lit up for reading
your battering *Dream* —
audible, deaf . . .
in another world then as now.
I used to want to live
to avoid your elegy.
Yet really we had the same life,
the generic one
our generation offered
(*Les Maudits* — the compliment
each American generation
pays itself in passing):
first students, then with our own,
our galaxy of grands maîtres,
our fifties' fellowships
to Paris, Rome and Florence,
veterans of the Cold War not the War —
all the best of life . . .
then daydreaming to drink at six,
waiting for the iced fire,
even the feel of the frosted glass,

like waiting for a girl . . .
if you had waited.
We asked to be obsessed with writing,
and we were.

Do you wake dazed like me,
and find your lost glasses in a shoe?
Something so heavy lies on my heart –
there, still here, the good days
when we sat by a cold lake in Maine,
talking about the *Winter's Tale*,
Leontes' jealousy
in Shakespeare's broken syntax.
You got there first.
Just the other day,
I discovered how we differ – humor . . .
even in this last *Dream Song*,
to mock your catlike flight
from home and classes –
to leap from the bridge.

Girls will not frighten the frost from the grave.

To my surprise, John,
I pray *to* not for you,
think of you not myself,
smile and fall asleep.

156   ROBERT LOWELL (1917–1977)

STRANGERS

THE WORLD STATE

Oh, how I love Humanity,
　　With love so pure and pringlish,
And how I hate the horrid French,
　　Who never will be English!

The International Idea,
　　The largest and the clearest,
Is welding all the nations now,
　　Except the one that's nearest.

This compromise has long been known,
　　This scheme of partial pardons,
In ethical societies
　　And small suburban gardens –

The villas and the chapels where
　　I learned with little labour
The way to love my fellow-man
　　and hate my next-door neighbour.

G. K. CHESTERTON (1874–1936)

THE STRANGER

Careless how it struck those nearest to him,
whose inquiring he'd no longer brook,
once more he departed; lost, forsook. –
For such nights of travel always drew him
stronglier than any lover's night.
How he'd watched in slumberless delight
out beneath the shining stars all yonder
circumscribed horizons roll asunder,
ever-changing like a changing fight;

others, with their moon-bright hamlets tendered
like some booty they had seized, surrendered
peacefully, or through tall trees would shed
glimpses of far-stretching parks, containing
grey ancestral houses that with craning
head a moment he inhabited,
knowing more deeply one could never bide;
then, already round the next curve speeding,
other highways, bridges, landscapes, leading
on to cities darkness magnified.

And to let all this, without all craving,
slip behind him meant beyond compare
more to him than pleasure, goods, or fame.
Though the well-steps in some foreign square,
daily hollowed by the drawers there,
seemed at times like something he could claim.

R. M. RILKE (1875–1926),
TRANS. J. B. LEISHMAN

THE LONELY MAN

A cat sits on the pavement by the house.
It lets itself be touched, then slides away.
A girl goes by in a hood; the winter noon's
Long shadows lengthen. The cat is gray,
It sits there. It sits there all day, every day.

A collie bounds into my arms: he is a dog
And, therefore, finds nothing human alien.
He lives at the preacher's with a pair of cats.
The soft half-Persian sidles to me;
Indoors, the old white one watches blindly.

How cold it is! Some snow slides from a roof
When a squirrel jumps off it to a squirrel-proof
Feeding-station; and, a lot and two yards down,
A fat spaniel snuffles out to me
And sobers me with his untrusting frown.

He worries about his yard: past it, it's my affair
If I halt Earth in her track – his duty's done.
And the cat and the collie worry about the old one:
They come, when she's out too, so uncertainly . . .
It's my block; I know them, just as they know me.

As for the others, those who wake up every day
And feed these, keep the houses, ride away
To work – I don't know them, they don't know me.
Are we friends or enemies? Why, who can say?
We nod to each other sometimes, in humanity,

Or search one another's faces with a yearning
Remnant of faith that's almost animal. . . .
The gray cat that just sits there: surely it is learning
To be a man; will find, soon, *some especial
Opening in a good firm for a former cat.*

THESE STRANGERS,
IN A FOREIGN WORLD

These Strangers, in a foreign World,
Protection asked of me –
Befriend them, lest Yourself in Heaven
Be found a Refugee –

STRANGE MEETING

It seemed that out of battle I escaped
Down some profound dull tunnel, long since scooped
Through granites which titanic wars had groined.
Yet also there encumbered sleepers groaned,
Too fast in thought or death to be bestirred.
Then, as I probed them, one sprang up, and stared
With piteous recognition in fixed eyes,
Lifting distressful hands as if to bless.
And by his smile I knew that sullen hall,
By his dead smile I knew we stood in Hell.
With a thousand pains that vision's face was grained;
Yet no blood reached there from the upper ground,
And no guns thumped, or down the flues made moan.
'Strange friend,' I said 'here is no cause to mourn.'
'None,' said the other, 'save the undone years,
The hopelessness. Whatever hope is yours,
Was my life also; I went hunting wild
After the wildest beauty in the world,
Which lies not calm in eyes, or braided hair,
But mocks the steady running of the hour,
And if it grieves, grieves richlier than here.
For by my glee might many men have laughed,
And of my weeping something had been left,
Which must die now. I mean the truth untold,
The pity of war, the pity war distilled.

Now men will go content with what we spoiled,
Or, discontent, boil bloody, and be spilled.
They will be swift with swiftness of the tigress,
None will break ranks, though nations trek from
      progress.
Courage was mine, and I had mystery,
Wisdom was mine, and I had mastery:
To miss the march of this retreating world
Into vain citadels that are not walled.
Then, when much blood had clogged their
      chariot-wheels,
I would go up and wash them from sweet wells,
Even with truths that lie too deep for taint.
I would have poured my spirit without stint
But not through wounds; not on the cess of war.
Foreheads of men have bled where no wounds were.
I am the enemy you killed, my friend.
I knew you in this dark: for so you frowned
Yesterday through me as you jabbed and killed.
I parried; but my hands were loath and cold.
Let us sleep now . . .'

KARMA

Christmas was in the air and all was well
With him, but for a few confusing flaws
In divers of God's images. Because
A friend of his would neither buy nor sell,
Was he to answer for the axe that fell?
He pondered; and the reason for it was,
Partly, a slowly freezing Santa Claus
Upon the corner, with his beard and bell.

Acknowledging an improvident surprise,
He magnified a fancy that he wished
The friend whom he had wrecked were here again.
Not sure of that, he found a compromise;
And from the fulness of his heart he fished
A dime for Jesus who had died for men.

E. A. ROBINSON (1869–1935)

PROVIDE, PROVIDE

The witch that came (the withered hag)
To wash the steps with pail and rag
Was once the beauty Abishag,

The picture pride of Hollywood.
Too many fall from great and good
For you to doubt the likelihood.

Die early and avoid the fate.
Or if predestined to die late,
Make up your mind to die in state.

Make the whole stock exchange your own!
If need be occupy a throne,
Where nobody can call *you* crone.

Some have relied on what they knew,
Others on being simply true.
What worked for them might work for you.

No memory of having starred
Atones for later disregard
Or keeps the end from being hard.

Better to go down dignified
With boughten friendship at your side
Than none at all. Provide, provide!

ROBERT FROST (1874–1963)

BEST SOCIETY

When I was a child, I thought,
Casually, that solitude
Never needed to be sought.
Something everybody had,
Like nakedness, it lay at hand,
Not specially right or specially wrong,
A plentiful and obvious thing
Not at all hard to understand.

Then, after twenty, it became
At once more difficult to get
And more desired – though all the same
More undesirable; for what
You are alone has, to achieve
The rank of fact, to be expressed
In terms of others, or it's just
A compensating make-believe.

Much better stay in company!
To love you must have somone else,
Giving requires a legatee,
Good neighbours need whole parishfuls
Of folk to do it on – in short,
Our virtues are all social; if,
Deprived of solitude, you chafe,
It's clear you're not the virtuous sort.

Viciously, then, I lock my door.
The gas-fire breathes. The wind outside
Ushers in evening rain. Once more
Uncontradicting solitude
Supports me on its giant palm;
And like a sea-anemone
Or simple snail, there cautiously
Unfolds, emerges, what I am.

THE GUEST

Who is the guest? *I* was one among *you*.
Each guest is *more*, though, when his hour begins;
for out of guesting's oldest origins
something unknown is potent in him too.

He comes and goes. He has no permanence.
Yet, feeling sudden shelteredness extend,
midway between a stranger and a friend
he rests in equipoised benevolence.

172   R. M. RILKE (1875–1926),
TRANS. J. B. LEISHMAN

TO HIS FRIEND TO AVOID
CONTENTION OF WORDS

Words beget Anger: Anger brings forth blows:
Blows make of dearest friends immortal Foes.
For which prevention (Sociate) let there be
Betwixt us two no more *Logomachie.*
Far better 'twere for either to be mute,
Than for to murder friendship, by dispute.

TO A FALSE FRIEND

Our hands have met, but not our hearts;
Our hands will never meet again.
Friends, if we have ever been,
Friends we cannot now remain:
I only know I loved you once,
I only know I loved in vain;
Our hands have met, but not our hearts;
Our hands will never meet again!

Then farewell to heart and hand!
I would our hands had never met:
Even the outward form of love
Must be resign'd with some regret.
Friends, we still might seem to be,
If I my wrong could e'er forget;
Our hands have join'd but not our hearts:
I would our hands had never met!

174 THOMAS HOOD (1799–1845)

A LIGHT WOMAN

So far as our story approaches the end,
    Which do you pity the most of us three? –
My friend, or the mistress of my friend
    With her wanton eyes, or me?

My friend was already too good to lose,
    And seemed in the way of improvement yet,
When she crossed his path with her hunting-noose
    And over him drew her net.

When I saw him tangled in her toils,
    A shame, said I, if she adds just him
To her nine-and-ninety other spoils,
    The hundredth for a whim!

And before my friend be wholly hers,
    How easy to prove to him, I said,
An eagle's the game her pride prefers,
    Though she snaps at a wren instead!

So, I gave her eyes my own eyes to take,
    My hand sought hers as in earnest need,
And round she turned for my noble sake,
    And gave me herself indeed.

The eagle am I, with my fame in the world,
    The wren is he, with his maiden face.
– You look away and your lip is curled?
    Patience, a moment's space!

For see, my friend goes shaking and white;
    He eyes me as the basilisk:
I have turned, it appears, his day to night,
    Eclipsing his sun's disk.

And I did it, he thinks, as a very thief:
    'Though I love her – that, he comprehends –
One should master one's passions (love, in chief),
    And be loyal to one's friends!'

And she – she lies in my hand as tame
    As a pear late basking over a wall;
Just a touch to try and off it came;
    'Tis mine – can I let it fall?

With no mind to eat it, that's the worst!
    Were it thrown in the road, would the case assist?
'Twas quenching a dozen blue-flies' thirst
    When I gave its stalk a twist.

And I – what I seem to my friend, you see:
  What I soon shall seem to his love, you guess:
What I seem to myself, do you ask of me?
  No hero, I confess.

'Tis an awkward thing to play with souls,
  And matter enough to save one's own.
Yet think of my friend, and the burning coals
  He played with for bits of stone!

One likes to show the truth for the truth;
  That the woman was light is very true:
But suppose she says – Never mind that youth!
  What wrong have I done to you?

Well, any how, here the story stays,
  So far at least as I understand;
And, Robert Browning, you writer of plays,
  Here's a subject made to your hand!

WEST LONDON

Crouch'd on the pavement close by Belgrave Square,
A tramp I saw, ill, moody, and tongue-tied;
A babe was in her arms, and at her side
A girl; their clothes were rags, their feet were bare.

Some labouring men, whose work lay
    somewhere there,
Pass'd opposite; she touch'd her girl, who hied
Across, and begg'd, and came back satisfied.
The rich she had let pass with frozen stare.

Thought I: Above her state this spirit towers;
She will not ask of aliens, but of friends,
Of sharers in a common human fate.

She turns from that cold succour, which attends
The unknown little from the unknowing great,
And points us to a better time than ours.

IN THE NIGHT

I longed for companionship rather,
But my companions I always wished farther.
And now in the desolate night
I think only of the people I should like to bite.

STEVIE SMITH (1902–1971)

ABSENT FRIENDS

FRIENDSHIP

It is the awaited hour
over the table falls
interminably
the lamp's spread hair
Night turns the window to immensity
There is no one here
presence without name surrounds me

OCTAVIO PAZ (1914–   ),
TRANS. CHARLES TOMLINSON

THE MILL

The spoiling daylight inched along the bar-top,
Orange and cloudy, slowly igniting lint,
And then that glow was gone, and still your voice,
Serene with failure and with the ease of dying,
Rose from the shades that more and more became you.
Turning among its images, your mind
Produced the names of streets, the exact look
Of lilacs, 1903, in Cincinnati,
– Random, as if your testament were made,
The round sums all bestowed, and now you spent
Your pocket change, so as to be rid of it.
Or was it that you half-hoped to surprise
Your dead life's sound and sovereign anecdote?
What I remember best is the wrecked mill
You stumbled on in Tennessee; or was it
Somewhere down in Brazil? It slips my mind
Already. But there it was in a still valley
Far from the towns. No road or path came near it.
If there had been a clearing now it was gone,
And all you found amidst the choke of green
Was three walls standing, hurdled by great vines
And thatched by height on height of hushing leaves.
But still the mill-wheel turned! its crazy buckets
Creaking and lumbering out of the clogged race
And sounding, as you said, as if you'd found

Time all alone and talking to himself
In his eternal rattle.
                    How should I guess
Where they are gone to, now that you are gone,
Those fading streets and those most fragile lilacs,
Those fragmentary views, those times of day?
All that I can be sure of is the mill-wheel.
It turns and turns in my mind, over and over.

TO MR I. L.

Of that short Roll of friends writ in my heart
    Which with thy name begins, since their depart,
Whether in the English Provinces they be,
    Or drink of Po, Sequan, or Danubie,
There's none that sometimes greets us not, and yet
    Your Trent is Lethe; that past, you us forget.
You do not duties of Societies,
    If from th'embrace of a lov'd wife you rise,
View your fat Beasts, stretch'd Barns,
      and labour'd fields,
    Eat, play, ride, take all joys which all day yields,
And then again to your embracements go:
    Some hours on us your friends, and some bestow
Upon your Muse, else both we shall repent,
    I that my love, she that her gifts on you are spent.

SEA CANES

Half my friends are dead.
I will make you new ones, said earth.
No, give me them back, as they were, instead,
with faults and all, I cried.

Tonight I can snatch their talk
from the faint surf's drone
through the canes, but I cannot walk

on the moonlit leaves of ocean
down that white road alone,
or float with the dreaming motion

of owls leaving earth's load.
O earth, the number of friends you keep
exceeds those left to be loved.

The sea canes by the cliff flash green and silver;
they were the seraph lances of my faith,
but out of what is lost grows something stronger

that has the rational radiance of stone,
enduring moonlight, further than despair,
strong as the wind, that through dividing canes
brings those we love before us, as they were,
with faults and all, not nobler, just there.

DEREK WALCOTT (1930–   )   187

19 OCTOBER

The woods have cast their crimson foliage,
The faded field is silvery with frost;
The sun no sooner glimmers than it's lost
Behind drab hills; the world's a hermitage.
Burn brightly, pine-logs, in my lonely cell;
And you, wine, friend to chilly autumn days,
Pour into me a comfortable haze,
Brief respite from the torments of my soul.

Perhaps some friend is driving up by stealth,
Hoping to surprise me; his face will press
Against my window; I'll rush out, embrace
Him warmly, from the heart, then drink his health
And talk, and laugh away our separation
Till dawn. I drink alone; no one will come;
The friends who crowd around me in this room
Are phantoms born of my imagination.

I drink alone, while on the Neva's banks
My comrades speak my name, propose a toast . . .
And who besides myself has missed the feast?
Are there not other spaces in your ranks?
Who else betrays the ritual gathering?
Who has been snatched away by the cold world?
Whose voice is silent when the roll is called?
Who has not come? Who's absent from the ring?

Our curly-headed songster is not there,
With his sweet-tuned guitar and blazing eyes;
Beneath fair myrtles and Italian skies
He calmly sleeps; and on his sepulchre
No friendly chisel has cut out a verse
In Russian, which some stranger in exile
Who wanders there might see, and pause awhile
To mourn a fellow-countryman's resting-place.

And are you seated at the gathering,
Horizon-seeker, you unresting soul,
Or are you off again, for the north pole
And the hot tropics? Pleasant voyaging!
I'm envious of you! Ever since you strode
Out of the school-gates, smiling, and leapt on
The first convenient ship, you've been the son
Of waves and storms, the sea has been your road.

Yet in your wanderings you have faithfully
Preserved the spirit of our boyhood years:
Amid the gales still echoed in your ears
The shouts and merriment of Tsarskoye;
You stretch a hand to us, we know we ride
Safe in your heart wherever you may sail;
And I recall your words? 'It's possible
Our fate is to be scattered far and wide!'

How excellent our union is, how rare!
Beating with one pulse still, as when we first
Linked fast in love, by friendly muses nursed;
In perfect freedom, perfectly secure.
Wherever fate decrees that we must go,
Wherever fortune leads us by the hand,
We're still the same: the world a foreign land,
Our mother country – Tsarskoye Selo.

From place to place driven by the storm, and caught
In nets of a harsh fate, I sought to rest
My weary head upon new friendship's breast,
And trembled when I found what I had sought.
But I deceived myself; for though I gave
My heart with all the ardency of youth,
Bitterly I found that trust, and truth,
Were far away in Petersburg, or the grave.

And then, here in this haunt of freezing winds
And blizzards, hope renewed itself, I found
Green shoots emerging from the stony ground;
A brief, sweet solace. Three of you, dear friends,
I embraced here! I could not speak for joy
When you, first, Pushchin, called on me, and chased
Away the dismal thoughts of a disgraced
Poet, as once you cheered a lonely boy.

And you, whom fortune always blessed, I greet you,
Dear Gorchakov! The frigid glare of fame
Has not impaired your heart; you are the same
Free spirit, loyal to your friends and virtue.
Widely divergent are the paths we trace;
Life early separated us; and yet,
When on a country road by chance we met,
There was a brother's warmth in your embrace.

When I was envious even of the shades
Who share my house, since every face had turned
Against me, even my family, I yearned
For you, enchanter of Permessian maids,
My Delvig – and you came, amazingly!
You child of inspired indolence, your voice
Re-kindled fires and made my heart rejoice
At the benevolence of my destiny.

The spirit of song was present in us both,
We shared its agitation and delight
When we were young; two muses paused in flight
And lit on us, nursing each tender growth.
But I grew greedy for applause; your pride
Made you sing for the muses and your soul;
I squandered my whole life, a prodigal;
In quietness your talents multiplied.

The muses won't allow frivolity,
To serve the beautiful one must be sober.
But April's whisper is not like October,
Worldly desires work on us devilishly . . .
We try to call a halt – but it's too late!
We turn round, try to find our lost tracks through
The snow, but can't. That's how it was with you
And I, Wilhelm, my brother in art and fate!

It's time, it's time! The world's not worth the fret
Of all that hunting fever: come, Wilhelm,
Join me here where that fever can grow calm
In solitude. I wait for you; you're late –
Brighten my embers, let our discourse move
Like dawn across those wild Caucasian heights
You and I knew; and where a thought alights
Let's muse awhile – on Schiller, fame, or love.

For me, too, it is time ... My friends, feast well!
I will imagine mirth and revelry;
Moreover, here's a poet's prophecy:
One more swift year and I'll accept your call;
Everything I want will come to pass;
The months speed by – I'm at your celebrations!
How many tears! How many exclamations!
And lifted high, how many a brimming glass!

And first let's drink to us, our sparkling throng!
And when we've drunk, let's fill our glasses full
Once more, and drink a blessing on our school:
Bless it, triumphant muse – may it live long!
The teachers of that youthful brotherhood,
The dead, the living, we will honour them,
Pressing our grateful lips to the cool rim,
Recall no wrongs, but praise all that was good.

More wine, up to the brim! Our hearts on fire
For the next toast, let's raise the crimson glass!
Whom do we honour now? – but can't you guess?
That's right! Long live the Tsar! We toast the Tsar.
He is a man; confusions, passions, sway
His life like everyone's; he is the slave
Of the passing moment ... So, his crimes forgive:
He captured Paris, founded our Lycée.

Let us enjoy the feast while we are here!
Alas, our band has dwindled; one is sealed
In the black grave, one's wandering in far fields;
Fate glances, drops her gaze ... we disappear;
The days flash by, in one year we have grown
Unnoticeably closer to our end ...
Which one of us, in his old age, my friends,
Will celebrate the founding day alone?

Sad guest of those who will not understand
His tedious words, who barely suffer him,
He will recall us and, his eyes grown dim,
To heavy lids will lift a trembling hand ...
May he, too, find a poignant consolation
And drink to our friendship in the cup of wine,
As now, in this disgraced retreat of mine,
I've drowned my sadness in your celebration.

194   ALEXANDER PUSHKIN (1799–1837),
TRANS. D. M. THOMAS

AS THROUGH THE WILD
GREEN HILLS OF WYRE
From A SHROPSHIRE LAD

As through the wild green hills of Wyre
The train ran, changing sky and shire,
And far behind, a fading crest,
Low in the forsaken west
Sank the high-reared head of Clee,
My hand lay empty on my knee.
Aching on my knee it lay:
That morning half a shire away
So many an honest fellow's fist
Had well-nigh wrung it from the wrist.
Hand, said I, since now we part
From fields and men we know by heart,
For strangers' faces, strangers' lands, –
Hand, you have held true fellows' hands.
Be clean then; rot before you do
A thing they'd not believe of you.
You and I must keep from shame
In London streets the Shropshire name;
On banks of Thames they must not say
Severn breeds worse men than they;
And friends abroad must bear in mind
Friends at home they leave behind.
Oh, I shall be stiff and cold

When I forget you, hearts of gold;
The land where I shall mind you not
Is the land where all's forgot.
And if my foot returns no more
To Teme nor Corve nor Severn shore,
Luck, my lads, be with you still
By falling stream and standing hill,
By chiming tower and whispering tree,
Men that made a man of me.
About your work in town and farm
Still you'll keep my head from harm,
Still you'll help me, hands that gave
A grasp to friend me to the grave.

MR FLOOD'S PARTY

Old Eben Flood, climbing alone one night
Over the hill between the town below
And the forsaken upland hermitage
That held as much as he should ever know
On earth again of home, paused warily.
The road was his with not a native near;
And Eben, having leisure, said aloud,
For no man else in Tilbury Town to hear:

'Well, Mr Flood, we have the harvest moon
Again, and we may not have many more;
The bird is on the wing, the poet says,
And you and I have said it here before.
Drink to the bird.' He raised up to the light
The jug that he had gone so far to fill,
And answered huskily: 'Well, Mr Flood,
Since you propose it, I believe I will.'

Alone, as if enduring to the end
A valiant armour of scarred hopes outworn,
He stood there in the middle of the road
Like Roland's ghost winding a silent horn.
Below him, in the town among the trees,
Where friends of other days had honoured him,
A phantom salutation of the dead
Rang thinly till old Eben's eyes were dim.

Then as a mother lays her sleeping child
Down tenderly, fearing it may awake,
He set the jug down slowly at his feet
With trembling care, knowing that most things break;
And only when assured that on firm earth
It stood, as the uncertain lives of men
Assuredly did not, he paced away,
And with his hand extended paused again:

'Well, Mr Flood, we have not met like this
In a long time; and many a change has come
To both of us, I fear, since last it was
We had a drop together. Welcome home!'
Convivially returning with himself,
Again he raised the jug up to the light;
And with an acquiescent quaver said:
'Well, Mr Flood, if you insist, I might.

'Only a very little, Mr Flood –
For auld lang syne. No more, sir; that will do.'
So, for the time, apparently it did,
And Eben evidently thought so too;
For soon amid the silver loneliness
Of night he lifted up his voice and sang,
Secure, with only two moons listening,
Until the whole harmonious landscape rang –

'For auld lang syne.' The weary throat gave out,
The last word wavered, and the song was done.
He raised again the jug regretfully
And shook his head, and was again alone.
There was not much that was ahead of him,
And there was nothing in the town below –
Where strangers would have shut the many doors
That many friends had opened long ago.

E. A. ROBINSON (1869–1935)

THE UNSEEN PLAYMATE

When children are playing alone on the green,
In comes the playmate that never was seen.
When children are happy and lonely and good,
The Friend of the Children comes out of the wood.

Nobody heard him and nobody saw,
His is a picture you never could draw,
But he's sure to be present, abroad or at home,
When children are happy and playing alone.

He lies in the laurels, he runs on the grass,
He sings when you tinkle the musical glass;
Whene'er you are happy and cannot tell why,
The Friend of the Children is sure to be by!

He loves to be little, he hates to be big,
'Tis he that inhabits the caves that you dig;
'Tis he when you play with your soldiers of tin
That sides with the Frenchmen and never can win.

'Tis he, when at night you go off to your bed,
Bids you go to your sleep and not trouble your head;
For wherever they're lying, in cupboard or shelf,
'Tis he will take care of your playthings himself!

200   ROBERT LOUIS STEVENSON (1850–1894)

BLUE HILLS OVER THE NORTH WALL

Blue hills over the north wall;
White water swirling to the east of the city:
This is where you must leave me –
A long puff of thistledown
    on a thousand mile journey.
Ah the drifting clouds
    and the thoughts of a wanderer!
The setting sun
    and emotions of old friends.
A wave of the hand now
    and you are gone.
Our horses whinnied to each other at parting.

LI PO (AD 701–762),
TRANS. INNES HERDON

FAREWELL

What? to have had gas, and to expect
No more than a week's sick, and to get Blighty –
This is the gods' gift and not anyway exact
To Ypres, or bad St Julien or Somme Farm.
Don Hancocks, shall I no more see your face frore,
Gloucester-good, in the first light? (But you are dead!)
Shall I see no more Monger with india-rubber
Twisted face? (But machine-gun caught him
        and his grimace.)
No more to march happy with such good comrades,
Watching the sky, the brown land, the bayonet blades
Moving – to muse on music forgetting the pack.
Nor to hear Gloucester with Stroud debating the lack
Of goodliness or virtue in girls on farmlands.
Nor to hear Cheltenham hurling at Cotswold demands
Of civilization; nor west Severn joking at east Severn?
No more, across the azure or brown lands,
The morning mist or high day clear of rack,
Shall move my dear knees, or feel them frosted,
        shivering
By Somme or Aubers – or to have a courage from faces
Full of all west England. Her God gives graces.
There was not one of all that battalion
Loved his comrades as well as I – but kept shy.
Or said in verse, what his voice would not rehearse.

So, gassed, I went back to northlands
    where voices speak soft as in verse.
And, after, to meet evil not fit for the thought one
    touch to dwell on.

Dear battalion, the dead of you would not have let
Your comrade be so long prey for the unquiet
Black evil of the unspoken and concealed pit.
You would have had me safe – dead or free happy alive.

They bruise my head and torture
    with their own past-hate
Sins of the past, and lie so as earth moves at it.
You dead ones – I lay with you under
    the unbroken wires once.

FLETCHER'S LAMENT FOR HIS FRIEND

Come, sorrow, come! bring all thy cries,
All thy laments, and all thy weeping eyes!
Burn out, you living monuments of woe!
Sad, sullen griefs, now rise and overflow!
      Virtue is dead;
      Oh! cruel fate!
      All youth is fled;
      All our laments too late.
Oh, noble youth, to thy ne'er dying name,
Oh, happy youth, to thy still growing fame,
To thy long peace in earth, this sacred knell
Our last loves ring – farewell, farewell, farewell!
Go, happy soul, to thy eternal birth!
And press his body lightly, gentle Earth.

TO E. T.: 1917

You sleep too well – too far away,
    For sorrowing word to soothe or wound;
Your very quiet seems to say
    How longed-for a peace you have found.

Else, had not death so lured you on,
    You would have grieved – 'twixt joy and fear –
To know how my small loving son
    Had wept for you, my dear.

FELIX RANDAL

Felix Randal the farrier, O he is dead then?
    my duty all ended,
Who have watched his mould of man,
    big-boned and hardy-handsome
Pining, pining, till time when reason rambled
    in it and some
Fatal four disorders, fleshed there, all contended?

Sickness broke him. Impatient he cursed at first,
    but mended
Being anointed and all; though a heavenlier heart
    began some
Months earlier, since I had our sweet reprieve
    and ransom
Tendered to him. Ah well, God rest him all road
    ever he offended!

This seeing the sick endears them to us,
    us too it endears.
My tongue had taught thee comfort,
    touch had quenched thy tears,
Thy tears that touched my heart, child, Felix,
    poor Felix Randal;

How far from then forethought of,
    all thy more boisterous years,
When thou at the random grim forge,
    powerful amidst peers,
Didst fettle for the great grey drayhorse his bright
    and battering sandal!

LEAN GAIUS, WHO WAS
THINNER THAN A STRAW

Lean Gaius, who was thinner than a straw
And who could slip through even a locked door,
Is dead, and we his friends are twice bereft,
In losing him and finding nothing left
To put into the coffin: what they'll do
In Hades with a creature who is too
Shadowy to be a Shade, God knows,
But when we bear him to his last repose,
We'll make it stylish – mourners, black crêpe, bier,
The lot, and though he won't himself appear,
His empty coffin's progress will be pious –
THE DEATH OF NOTHING, FUNERAL OF GAIUS!

ON THE DEATH OF
COUNTESS LUISE SCHWERIN

I

Many a legend I have meditated,
searching for the shining name of you.
Like those nights when summer's reinstated
and our earth become enconstellated,
all things to yourself you have related,
and surround me like a deepest blue.

For those gazers, though, that never met you
all that I can do is leave in all
other things a space that will inset you,
just as in your sketching days they let you
leave a whiteness for the waterfall.

That is all I'll leave for them, while I
hide myself among the least and nearest.
Portraiture would let too much go by.
You are deepest background, clearest sky,
softly framed by objects that were dearest.

II

Lovers, sufferers, like those unstaying
leaves within the fading park blew past.
Something, though, like tapestry's displaying
even yet your walking and your praying,
and the quiet colours still are fast.

All is visible: eyes' delectation
(where a day of spring is holding fête),
guarded head-band of your jubilation,
and, alone, your pride's small vineyard gate
to the long road through your tribulation.

In each picture, though, untouched by years,
white, and always in the same unending
white, and on no other sign depending,
your love's soothing figure re-appears,
as to proffer something lightly bending.

210   R. M. RILKE (1875–1926),
        TRANS. J. B. LEISHMAN

TO THE MEMORY OF MR. OLDHAM

Farewell, too little and too lately known,
Whom I began to think and call my own:
For sure our Souls were near alli'd, and thine
Cast in the same poetick mold with mine.
One common Note on either Lyre did strike,
And Knaves and Fools we both abhorr'd alike.
To the same Goal did both our Studies drive:
The last set out the soonest did arrive.
Thus *Nisus* fell upon the slippery place,
Whilst his young Friend perform'd and won the Race.
O early ripe! to thy abundant Store
What could advancing Age have added more?
It might (what Nature never gives the Young)
Have taught the Numbers of thy Native Tongue.
But Satire needs not those, and Wit will shine
Through the harsh Cadence of a rugged Line.

A noble Error, and but seldom made,
When Poets are by too much force betray'd.
Thy gen'rous Fruits, though gather'd ere their prime,
Still shew'd a Quickness; and maturing Time
But mellows what we write to
        the dull Sweets of Rhyme.
Once more, hail, and farewell! farewell, thou young,
But ah! too short, *Marcellus* of our Tongue!
Thy Brows with Ivy and with Laurels bound;
But Fate and gloomy Night encompass thee around.

YORK: IN MEMORIAM W. H. AUDEN

The butterflies of northern England
    dance above the goosefoot
below the brick wall of a dead factory.
    After Wednesday
comes Thursday, and so on. The sky breathes heat;
the fields burn. The towns give off a smell of striped
cloth, long-wrapped and musty; dahlias die of thirst.
And your voice – 'I have known
    three great poets. Each
one a prize son of a bitch' – sounds in my ears
with disturbing clarity. I slow my steps

and turn to look round. Four years soon
since you died in an Austrian hotel.
    Under the crossing sign
not a soul: tiled roofs, asphalt, limestone,
poplars. Chester died, too – you know that
only too well. Like beads on a dusty abacus,
sparrows sit solemnly on wires. Nothing so much
transforms a familiar entrance into a crowd of columns
as love for a man, especially when

he's dead. The absence of wind compels taut leaves
to tense their muscles and stir against their will.
The white butterflies' dance is like a storm-tossed ship.
A man takes his own blind alley with him
        wherever he goes
about the world; and a bent knee, with its obtuse angle,
multiplies the captive perspective,
like a wedge of cranes holding their course
for the south. Like all things moving onward.

The emptiness, swallowing sunlight –
        something in common with
the hawthorn – grows steadily more palpable
in the outstretched hand's direction, and
the world merges into a long street where others live.
In this sense, it is England. England, in this sense,
still an empire and fully capable – if
you believe the music gurgling like water –
of ruling waves. Or any element, for that matter.

Lately, I've been losing my grip a little: snarl
at my shopwindow reflection; while my finger
dials its number, my hand lets the phone fall.
Closing my eyes, I see an empty boat,
motionless, far out in the bay.
Coming out of the phone booth,

I hear a starling's voice – in its cry alarm.
But before it flies away the sound

melts in the air. Whose blue expanse,
    innocent of objects,
is much like this life here
    (where things stand out more in the desert),
for you're not here. And vacuum gradually
fills the landscape. Like flecks of foam,
sheep take their ease on bottle-green waves
of Yorkshire heather. The corps de ballet of nimble
butterflies, taking their cue from an unseen bow,
flicker above a grass-grown ditch, giving the eye

no point of rest And the willow herb's vertical stalk
is longer than the ancient Roman road,
heading north, forgotten by all at Rome.
Subtracting the greater from the lesser –
    time from man –
you get words, the remainder,
    standing out against their
white background more clearly than the body
ever manages to while it lives, though it cry
    'Catch me!'–

thus the source of love turns into the object of love.

JOSEPH BRODSKY (1940–   )   215

LOOKING BACK

TAM CARI CAPITIS

That the world will never be quite –
    what a cliché – the same again
Is what we only learn by the event
When a friend dies out on us and is not there
To share the periphery of a remembered scent

Or leave his thumb-print on a shared ideal;
Yet it is not at floodlit moments we miss him most,
Not intervolution of wind-rinsed plumage of oatfield
Nor curragh dancing off a primeval coast

Nor the full strings of passion; it is in killing
Time where he could have livened it,
    such as the drop-by-drop
Of games like darts or chess, turning the faucet
On full at a threat to the queen or double top.

HERACLITUS

They told me, Heraclitus, they told me you were dead,
They brought me bitter news to hear
    and bitter tears to shed.
I wept, as I remembered, how often you and I
Had tired the sun with talking and sent him
    down the sky.

And now that thou art lying, my dear old Carian guest,
A handful of grey ashes, long, long ago at rest,
Still are thy pleasant voices, thy nightingales, awake;
For Death, he taketh all away, but them he cannot take.

220   WILLIAM JOHNSON CORY (1823–1892)

IF ANYBODY'S FRIEND BE DEAD

If anybody's friend be dead
It's sharpest of the theme
The thinking how they walked alive –
At such and such a time –

Their costume, of a Sunday,
Some manner of the Hair –
A prank nobody knew but them
Lost, in the Sepulchre –

How warm, they were, on such a day,
You almost feel the date –
So short way off it seems –
And now – they're Centuries from that –

How pleased they were, at what you said –
You try to touch the smile
And dip your fingers in the frost –
When was it – Can you tell –

You asked the Company to tea –
Acquaintance – just a few –
And chatted close with this Grand Thing
That don't remember you –

Past Bows, and Invitations –
Past Interview, and Vow –
Past what Ourself can estimate –
That – makes the Quick of Woe!

TWO FRIENDS

The last word this one spoke
was my name. The last word
that one spoke
was my name.

My two friends
had never met. But when they said
that last word
they spoke to each other.

I am proud to have given them a language
of one word, a narrow space
in which, without knowing it,
they met each other at last.

TO A FRIEND

When we were idlers with the loitering rills,
The need of human love we little noted:
Our love was nature; and the peace that floated
On the white mist, and dwelt upon the hills,
To sweet accord subdued our wayward wills:
One soul was ours, one mind, one heart devoted,
That, wisely doating, ask'd not why it doated,
And ours the unknown joy, which knowing kills.
But now I find, how dear thou wert to me;
That man is more than half of nature's treasure,
Of that fair Beauty which no eye can see,
Of that sweet music which no ear can measure;
And now the streams may sing for others' pleasure,
The hills sleep on in their eternity.

From ON THE DEATH OF
MR WILLIAM HERVEY

He was my *Friend*, the truest *Friend* on earth;
A strong and mighty *Influence* joyn'd our *Birth*.
Nor did we envy the most sounding *Name*
    By *Friendship* giv'n of old to *Fame*.
None but his *Brethren* he, and *Sisters* knew,
    Whom the kind youth preferr'd to Me:
    And ev'n in that we did agree,
For much above my self I lov'd them too.

Say, for you saw us, ye immortal *Lights*,
How oft unweari'd have we spent the Nights?
Till the *Ledaean Stars*, so fam'd for *Love*,
    Wondred at us from above.
We spent them not in toys, in lusts, or wine;
    But search of deep *Philosophy*,
    Wit, *Eloquence*, and *Poetry*,
Arts which I lov'd, for they, my *Friend*, were *Thine*.

Ye fields of *Cambridge*, our dear *Cambridge*, say,
Have ye not seen us walking every day?
Was there a *Tree* about which did not know
　　The *Love* betwixt us two?
Henceforth, ye gentle *Trees*, for ever fade;
　　Or your sad branches thicker joyn,
　　And into darksome shades combine,
Dark as the *Grave* wherein my *Friend* is laid.

THE OLD FAMILIAR FACES

I have had playmates, I have had companions,
In my days of childhood, in my joyful school-days,
All, all are gone, the old familiar faces.

I have been laughing, I have been carousing,
Drinking late, sitting late, with my bosom cronies,
All, all are gone, the old familiar faces.

I loved a love once, fairest among women:
Closed are her doors on me, I must not see her –
All, all are gone, the old familiar faces.

I have a friend, a kinder friend has no man;
Like an ingrate, I left my friend abruptly;
Left him, to muse on the old familiar faces.

Ghost-like I paced round the haunts of my childhood,
Earth seemed a desert I was bound to traverse,
Seeking to find the old familiar faces.

Friend of my bosom, thou more than a brother,
Why wert not thou born in my father's dwelling?
So might we talk of the old familiar faces —

How some they have died, and some they have left me,
And some are taken from me; all are departed;
All, all are gone, the old familiar faces.

DREAMING THAT I WENT WITH LI
AND YÜ TO VISIT YÜAN CHĒN
(Written in exile)

At night I dreamt I was back in Ch'ang-an;
I saw again the faces of old friends.
And in my dreams, under an April sky,
They led me by the hand to wander in the spring
     winds.
Together we came to the village of Peace and Quiet;
We stopped our horses at the gate of Yüan Chēn.
Yüan Chēn was sitting all alone;
When he saw me coming, a smile came to his face.
He pointed back at the flowers in the western court;
Then opened wine in the northern summer-house.
He seemed to be saying that neither of us had changed;
He seemed to be regretting that joy will not stay;
That our souls had met only for a little while,
To part again with hardly time for greeting.
I woke up and thought him still at my side;
I put out my hand; there was nothing there at all.

THE MEETING

After so long an absence
   At last we meet again:
Does the meeting give us pleasure,
   Or does it give us pain?

The tree of life has been shaken,
   And but few of us linger now,
Like the Prophet's two or three berries
   In the top of the uttermost bough.

We cordially greet each other
   In the old, familiar tone;
And we think, though we do not say it,
   How old and grey he is grown!

We speak of a Merry Christmas
   And many a Happy New Year;
But each in his heart is thinking
   Of those that are not here.

We speak of friends and their fortunes,
    And of what they did and said,
Till the dead alone seem living,
    And the living alone seem dead.

And at last we hardly distinguish
    Between the ghosts and the guests;
And a mist and shadow of sadness
    Steals over our merriest jests.

FELIX ANTONIUS
(After Martial)

To-day, my friend is seventy-five;
    He tells his tale with no regret;
    His brave old eyes are steadfast yet,
His heart the lightest heart alive.

He sees behind him green and wide
    The pathway of his pilgrim years;
    He sees the shore, and dreadless hears
The whisper of the creeping tide.

For out of all his days, not one
    Has passed and left its unlaid ghost
    To seek a light for ever lost,
Or wail a deed for ever done.

So for reward of life-long truth
    He lives again, as good men can,
    Redoubling his allotted span
With memories of a stainless youth.

THE WORD

My friend, my bonny friend, when we are old,
   And hand in hand go tottering down the hill,
May we be rich in love's refinèd gold,
   May love's gold coin be current with us still.

May love be sweeter for the vanished days,
   And your most perfect beauty still as dear
As when your troubled singer stood at gaze
   In the dear March of a most sacred year.

May what we are be all we might have been,
   And that potential, perfect, O my friend,
And may there still be many sheafs to glean
   In our love's acre, comrade, till the end.

And may we find when ended is the page
Death but a tavern on our pilgrimage.

JOHN MASEFIELD (1878–1967)

MAY AND DEATH

I wish that when you died last May,
  Charles, there had died along with you
Three parts of spring's delightful things;
  Ay, and, for me, the fourth part too.

A foolish thought, and worse, perhaps!
  There must be many a pair of friends
Who, arm in arm, deserve the warm
  Moon-births and the long evening-ends.

So, for their sake, be May still May!
  Let their new time, as mine of old,
Do all it did for me: I bid
  Sweet sights and sounds throng manifold.

Only, one little sight, one plant,
  Woods have in May, that starts up green
Save a sole streak which, so to speak,
  Is spring's blood, spilt its leaves between, –

That, they might spare; a certain wood
  Might miss the plant; their loss were small:
But I, – whene'er the leaf grows there,
  Its drop comes from my heart, that's all.

234   ROBERT BROWNING (1812–1889)

SCHOOLS AND SCHOOLFELLOWS

FLOREAT ETONA

Twelve years ago I made a mock
    Of filthy trades and traffics:
I wondered what they meant by stock;
    I wrote delightful sapphics;
I knew the streets of Rome and Troy,
    I supped with Fates and Furies, –
Twelve years ago I was a boy,
    A happy boy, at Drury's.

Twelve years ago! – how many a thought
    Of faded pains and pleasures
Those whispered syllables have brought
    From Memory's hoarded treasures!
The fields, the farms, the bats, the books,
    The glories and disgraces,
The voices of dear friends, the looks
    Of all familiar faces!

Kind *Mater* smiles again to me,
    As bright as when we parted;
I seem again the frank, the free,
    Stout-limbed, and simple-hearted!

Pursuing every idle dream,
    And shunning every warning;
With no hard work but Bovney stream,
    No chill except Long Morning:

Now stopping Harry Vernon's ball
    That rattled like a rocket;
Now hearing Wentworth's 'Fourteen all!'
    And striking for the pocket;

Now feasting on a cheese and flitch, –
    Now drinking from the pewter;
Now leaping over Chalvey ditch,
    Now laughing at my tutor.

Where are my friends? I am alone;
    No playmate shares my beaker:
Some lie beneath the churchyard stone,
    And some – before the Speaker;
And some compose a tragedy,
    And some compose a rondeau;
And some draw sword for Liberty,
    And some draw pleas for John Doe.

Tom Mill was used to blacken eyes
    Without the fear of sessions;
Charles Medlar loathed false quantities

As much as false professions;
Now Mill keeps order in the land,
   A magistrate pedantic;
And Medlar's feet repose unscanned
   Beneath the wide Atlantic.

Wild Nick, whose oaths made such a din,
   Does Dr. Martext's duty;
And Mullion, with that monstrous chin,
   Is married to a Beauty;
And Darrell studies, week by week,
   His Mant, and not his Manton;
And Ball, who was but poor in Greek,
   Is very rich at Canton.

And I am eight-and-twenty now; —
   The world's cold chains have bound me;
And darker shades are on my brow,
   And sadder scenes around me;
In Parliament I fill my seat,
   With many other noodles;
And lay my head in Jermyn Street
   And sip my hock at Boodle's.

But often when the cares of life
   Have sent my temples aching,
When visions haunt me of a wife,

When duns await my waking,
When Lady Jane is in a pet,
  Or Hoby in a hurry,
When Captain Hazard wins a bet,
  Or Beaulieu spoils a curry, –

For hours and hours I think and talk
  Of each remembered hobby;
I long to lounge in Poet's walk,
  To shiver in the Lobby;
I wish that I could run away
  From House, and Court, and Levée,
Where bearded men appear to-day
  Just Eton boys grown heavy, –

That I could bask in childhood's sun,
  And dance o'er childhood's roses,
And find huge wealth in one pound one,
  Vast wit in broken roses,
And play Sir Giles at Datchet Lane,
  And call the milk-maids Houris, –
That I could be a boy again, –
  A happy boy, – at Drury's.

OLD FRIENDS

The sky widens to Cornwall. A sense of sea
   Hangs in the lichenous branches
     and still there's light.
The road from its tunnel of blackthorn rises free
      To a final height,

And over the west is glowing a mackerel sky
   Whose opal fleece has faded to purple pink.
In this hour of the late-lit, listening evening, why
      Do my spirits sink?

The tide is high and a sleepy Atlantic sends
   Exploring ripple on ripple down Polzeath shore,
And the gathering dark is full of the thought of friends
     I shall see no more.

Where is Anne Channel who loved this place the best,
   With her tense blue eyes and her shopping-bag
     falling apart,
And her racy gossip and nineteen-twenty zest,
      And that warmth of heart?

Where's Roland, easing his most unwieldy car
    With its load of golf-clubs, backwards into the lane?
Where Kathleen Stokes with her Sealyhams? There's
        Doom Bar;
            Bray Hill shows plain;

For this is the turn, and the well-known trees
        draw near;
    On the road their pattern in moonlight fades
        and swells:
As the engine stops, from two miles off I hear
        St Minver bells.

What a host of stars in a wideness still and deep:
    What a host of souls, as a motor-bike whines away
And the silver snake of the estuary curls to sleep
        In Daymer Bay.

Are they one with the Celtic saints
        and the years between?
    Can they see the moonlit pools
        where ribbonweed drifts?
As I reach our hill, I am part of a sea unseen –
        The oppression lifts.

THE BROKEN FRIENDSHIP

'My heart is fallen in despair'
Said Easter Ross to Jolie Bear.
Jolie answered never a word
But passed her plate as if she had not heard.

Mrs Ross is took to her bed
And kept her eye fixed on the bed-rail peg
'When I am dead roll me under the barrow,
And who but pretty Jolie shall carry the harrow.'

Jolie Bear is gone away
Easter Ross's heart is broke,
Everything went out of her
When Jolie never spoke.

STEVIE SMITH (1902–1971)

IF MEMORY SERVES,
WE'VE SHARED TOGETHER

If memory serves, we've shared together
Thirty-four years, Julius. Weather
Both fair and foul as friends we've had,
Yet good times have outnumbered bad.
Indeed, if we were to divide
The days by pebbles – on one side
Black, on the other white – the higher
Heap would be bright. If you desire
To avoid the acid taste of life
And to be proof against the knife
That stabs the heart, follow my plan:
Don't come too close to any man.
That way your pleasure may be less,
So also will your bitterness.

PAYING CALLS

I went by footpath and by stile
    Beyond where bustle ends,
Strayed here a mile and there a mile
    And called upon some friends.

On certain ones I had not seen
    For years past did I call,
And then on others who had been
    The oldest friends of all.

It was the time of midsummer
    When they had used to roam;
But now, though tempting was the air,
    I found them all at home.

I spoke to one and other of them
    By mound and stone and tree
Of things we had done ere days were dim,
    But they spoke not to me.

THOMAS HARDY (1840–1928)   243

THE CHUMS

Some are in prison; some are dead;
    And none has read my books,
And yet my thought turns back to them,
    And I remember looks

Their sisters gave me, once or twice;
    But when I slowed my feet,
They taught me not to be too nice
    The way I tipped my hat.

And when I slipped upon the ice,
They saw that I fell more than twice.
    I'm grateful for that.

TO MY FRIENDS

Dear friends, and here I say friends
In the broad sense of the word:
Wife, sister, associates, relatives,
Schoolmates of both sexes,
People seen only once
Or frequented all my life;
Provided that between us, for at least a moment,
A line has been stretched,
A well-defined bond.

I speak for you, companions of a crowded
Road, not without its difficulties,
And for you too, who have lost
Soul, courage, the desire to live;
Or no one, or someone, or perhaps
        only one person, or you
Who are reading me: remember the time
Before the wax hardened,
When everyone was like a seal.
Each of us bears the imprint
Of a friend met along the way;
In each the trace of each.
For good or evil
In wisdom or in folly
Everyone stamped by everyone.

245

Now that time crowds in
And the undertakings are finished,
To all of you the humble wish
That autumn will be long and mild.

PRIMO LEVI (1919–1987),
TRANS. RUTH FELDMAN AND BRIAN SWANN

A LITTLE HEALTH

A little health,
A little wealth,
A little house and freedom,
And at the end
A little friend
And little cause to need him.

ANON
FROM THE DIARY OF FRANCIS KILVERT (1840–1879)

ACKNOWLEDGMENTS

Thanks are due to the following copyright holders for
permission to reprint:

AUDEN, W. H.: Faber and Faber Ltd and Random House, Inc
for, 'Thanksgiving for a Habitat IX' and 'For Friends Only'
from *Collected Poems*, ed. Edward Mendelson. Copyright © 1938
by W. H. Auden. Reprinted by permission of Random House,
Inc. BETJEMAN, JOHN: John Murray (Publishers) Ltd for, 'Old
Friends' from *Collected Poems*. BIERHORST, JOHN: Farrar, Straus
& Giroux, Inc for, 'Friendship' from *In the Trail of the Wind*.
© John Bierhorst, 1971. BRODSKY, JOSEPH: Farrar, Straus &
Giroux, Inc and Oxford University Press for, 'York': In
Memoriam W. H. Auden' from 'In England' from *A Part of
Speech*, tr. Alan Myers. Translation © 1980 by Farrar, Straus
& Giroux, Inc. Reprinted by permission of Farrar, Straus &
Giroux, Inc and by permission of Oxford University Press.
BROUGH, JOHN: Penguin Books Ltd for, 'This Life on Earth'
from *Poems from the Sanskrit*, tr. John Brough, Penguin
Classics, 1968. © John Brough, 1968. DE LA MARE, WALTER:
The Literary Trustees of Walter de la Mare, and the Society
of Authors as their representative for, 'The Feckless Dinner
Party', 'To E.T.' and 'In the Garden'. EWART, GAVIN: Random
House UK Ltd (Hutchinson) for, 'Office Friendships' from
The Collected Ewart 1933–1980. FROST, ROBERT: Random House
UK Ltd and Henry Holt and Co, Inc for, 'Mending Wall'. 'To
E.T.', 'A Time to Talk' and 'Provide Provide' from *The Poetry
of Robert Frost*, ed. Edward Connery Lathem. © 1964 by
Lesley Frost Ballantine. Copyright 1923 © 1969 by Henry
Holt and Co, Inc. GOGARTY, OLIVER ST. JOHN: Devin-Adair

248

INDEX OF FIRST LINES